"How can you cover your kids in pn shows us how in this practical thirty-(, and prayer prompts. She helps reader. ⌐ne who can transform a child's thoughts (head) and steps (feet) and all the tender places in between."

Jim Daly, president, Focus on the Family

"As parents, we desire the best for our children. But there are many times we feel at a loss for what to do, or we may wonder if we are doing enough to guide them toward a life lived for Jesus. It is too easy to forget the most powerful weapon we have: prayer! *Praying for Your Child from Head to Toe* is the guide I wish I'd had years ago but am so thankful exists today. I absolutely love this step-by-step daily journey of applying Scripture through prayer to all the different elements of our children's lives! This will be a resource I use over and over for years to come."

Ruth Schwenk, bestselling author of *Jesus, Calm My Heart* and *The Better Mom Devotional*

"We want to pray for our kids, but sometimes all that comes out is 'Lord, bless my child.' This book will show you from Scripture how to pray specifically and powerfully for your children in a whole new way. What an exciting opportunity we have as parents to pray for our kids. This book has jump-started my prayers as a mom, and I know it will do the same for you!"

Arlene Pellicane, speaker, author of *Parents Rising*, and host of the *Happy Home* podcast

"I would not be who I am today without the faithful prayers of my parents and grandparents. This is more than a book; it's a powerful way to love your children today and bless them tomorrow. There is no legacy more impactful or inheritance more valuable than the prayers said for us."

Holley Gerth, *Wall Street Journal*–bestselling author
of *What Your Mind Needs for Anxious Moments*

"Prayer is the work of a parent. From the moment your child is first embraced in your arms through their adult years, the one thing you can consistently do for them is pray. When you're at a loss for words, as we all are at different points of the parenting journey, this beautiful book will take you by the hand and lead the way."

Jill Savage, author of *Real Moms ... Real Jesus* and *No More Perfect Kids*

ep

estherpress

Books for Courageous Women

ESTHER PRESS VISION

*Publishing diverse voices that encourage and equip women to walk
courageously in the light of God's truth for such a time as this.*

BIBLICAL STATEMENT OF PURPOSE

*"For if you keep silent at this time, relief and deliverance will rise for the Jews from
another place, but you and your father's house will perish. And who knows whether
you have not come to the kingdom for such a time as this?"*

Esther 4:14 (ESV)

What people are saying about …

Praying
for Your Child
from Head to Toe

"In my early years as a mom, I learned that trusting God with my kids' lives would need to be an intentional daily decision. Praying for them became my way of reminding myself that God is in control and I am not. This beautiful collection of biblically based prayers is what I needed back then and can still utilize today as I continue to pray for my grown children and grandchildren. My dear friend Sharon is a gift to parents everywhere with this timely guide that will help you cover your kids from head to toe!

Lysa TerKeurst, #1 *New York Times*–bestselling author and president of Proverbs 31 Ministries

"If you know you should be praying for your children but don't exactly know where to start, this guided resource will be invaluable to you. Sharon Jaynes not only shows us why we should pray but also empowers us with specific areas to cover and creative ways to weave prayer into our ordinary days. Full of Scripture, examples, and encouragement, this practical tool will give you a renewed purpose and offer you an eternal perspective as a parent."

Karen Ehman, *New York Times*–bestselling author of *When Making Others Happy Is Making You Miserable* and international speaker

Sharon Jaynes

Praying
for Your Child
from Head to Toe

A 30-Day Guide to Powerful and
Effective Scripture-Based Prayers

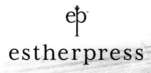

estherpress

Books for Courageous Women
from David C Cook

PRAYING FOR YOUR CHILD FROM HEAD TO TOE
Published by Esther Press,
an imprint of David C Cook
4050 Lee Vance Drive
Colorado Springs, CO 80918 U.S.A.

Integrity Music Limited, a Division of David C Cook
Brighton, East Sussex BN1 2RE, England

Unless otherwise noted, all Scripture quotations are taken from the Holy Bible, New
International Version®, NIV®. Copyright © 1973, 2011 by Biblica, Inc.™ Used by permission
of Zondervan. All rights reserved worldwide. www.zondervan.com. The "NIV" and "New
International Version" are trademarks registered in the United States Patent and Trademark
Office by Biblica, Inc. ™ Scripture quotations marked AMP are taken from the Amplified®
Bible (AMP), Copyright © 2015 by The Lockman Foundation. AMPC are taken from
the Amplified® Bible (AMPC), Copyright © 1954, 1987 by The Lockman Foundation.
Used by permission. www.lockman.org. ESV are taken from the ESV® Bible (The Holy
Bible, English Standard Version®), copyright © 2001 by Crossway, a publishing ministry
of Good News Publishers. Used by permission. All rights reserved; GNT are taken from
the Good News Translation in Today's English Version—Second Edition. Copyright ©
1992 by American Bible Society. Used by permission; NASB are taken from the (NASB®)
New American Standard Bible®, Copyright © 1960, 2020 by The Lockman Foundation.
Used by permission. All rights reserved. www.lockman.org; NCV are taken from the New
Century Version®. Copyright © 2005 by Thomas Nelson. Used by permission. All rights
reserved; NKJV are taken from the New King James Version®. Copyright © 1982 by Thomas
Nelson. Used by permission. All rights reserved; NLT are taken from the Holy Bible, New
Living Translation, copyright © 1996, 2015 by Tyndale House Foundation. Used by
permission of Tyndale House Publishers, Carol Stream, Illinois 60188. All rights reserved.
The author has added italics and bold to Scripture quotations for emphasis.

Library of Congress Control Number 2023935144
ISBN 978-0-8307-8590-2
eISBN 978-0-8307-8606-0

The Team: Susan McPherson, Michael Ross, Stephanie Bennett, Judy
Gillispie, Renée Chavez, James Hershberger, Susan Murdock
Cover Design: Emily Weigel

Printed in the United States of America
First Edition 2023

2 3 4 5 6 7 8 9 10 11

112223

To Steven
I thank God for the wonder of you.

Also available from Sharon Jaynes

*Praying for Your Husband from Head to Toe:
A Daily Guide to Scripture-Based Prayer*

Contents

Appendix

Part 1

The Power and Purpose of Prayer

Chapter 1

The Battle for Our Children

It was one of the most important days of my life. I knew it was coming, had nine months to prepare. But I had no idea the dramatic effect this one pivotal moment would have on my heart, my soul, my very being … forever.

After almost twenty-four hours of heaving and ho-ing, pushing and pulling, walking and waiting, nurses' cajoling and my husband's consoling, I gave one final push and Steven Hugh Jaynes Jr. came screeching into the world. Honestly, he didn't seem all that happy about it. With a squinched-up face and squalling protests, Steven seemed to be saying, "Put me back in there! I don't like it out here—and get that light out of my eyes!" Two tightly balled-up fists were ready to put up a fight to prove his point.

But when the nurses placed the cotton cap on his still-damp head, swaddled his fluid-covered body in a downy blanket, and nestled the squirming bundle on my chest, Steven surrendered his objections, melding into my body once again.

And I became a mother.

And I thought I was prepared.

And I was wrong.

My husband, Steve, and I had taken a six-week class at the local Red Cross on childcare, but the minute the nurse placed that little human on my chest, I knew motherhood was going to be very different from what I had experienced with that plastic doll. Steven was not made of durable plastic but delicate skin and breakable bones. He did not lie still when we tried to change his diaper but squirmed right out of those sticky tabs. I could not leave him on the counter for a fifteen-minute coffee break but had to give him constant attention. And the poop was real. And so was the love.

An inexplicable bond exists between a mother and her child. While the new life is being knit together in a mother's womb, her very blood is pumped from her heart to her child's. And even though the umbilical cord is cut in the delivery room, an invisible, indelible cord of love holds mother and child together for the rest of their lives. A quote attributed to Elizabeth Stone says it so well: "Making the decision to have a child is momentous. It is to decide forever to have your heart go walking around outside your body."

God has given moms the privilege and parental responsibility to shape and to mold not just another human being but an eternal soul, for a very short, very fleeting period of time. While our roles and responsibilities change throughout the stages from childhood through adulthood, one constant remains … prayer. And though hopefully our children will outlive us, they will never outlive our prayers that are etched in the heart of God.

The Power and Purpose of Prayer

Before we begin, let's look at the power and purpose of prayer. Prayer is an ongoing, continual conversation with God, acknowledging our total dependence on Him every moment of every day. It is not a way to twist God's arm to get Him to do what we want Him to do when we want Him to do it.

The purpose of prayer is to release God's power on earth as it is in heaven. It's not that God can't act without the prayers of His people. He can do anything He pleases (Psalm 115:3). However, He has established prayer as the gate through which His blessings flow. Charles Spurgeon called prayer "the sender nerve that moves the muscles of omnipotence."[1]

Prayer is not trying to pry God's blessings out of a stingy, relenting hand. He's not hoarding His favor, waiting for us to say the right words. Prayer is simply opening the storehouse of heaven for lavish blessings He already wants to give.

Scripture describes His love and His blessings as being "lavished" on us (Ephesians 1:7–8; 1 John 3:1). John wrote, "See what great love the Father has *lavished* on us, that we should be called children of God" (1 John 3:1a). He didn't simply use the word *given* but *lavished*. Webster defines *lavish* this way: "Given or provided with great generosity and abundance, to bestow with large generosity, profusion, a downpour."[2] Ponder those words separately.

Lavished.

Provided with great generosity.

Abundance.

Bestow with large generosity.

Profusion.

There's nothing stingy about that.

And while He longs to lavish us with His goodness, He often waits for us to ask. Jesus tells us that the Father knows what we need *before* we ask (Matthew 6:8); however, He waits for us to *pray and ask* before meeting the need (Matthew 7:7–8). James reminds us, "You do not have because you do not ask God" (James 4:2b). I am not saying I understand it fully. Prayer is simply the way God chose to engineer the flow of His power and activity from the spiritual realm into the physical realm. Prayer is the conduit through which God's power is released and His will is brought to earth as it is in heaven.

James wrote, "The prayer of a righteous person is powerful and effective" (James 5:16b). And if you know Jesus as Savior and Lord, then you are righteous and holy because of what He has done for you and in you (1 Corinthians 1:30). *Your* prayers are powerful and effective!

Prayer is not a means of *gaining control* over our children, to whip them into shape and make them the men and women *we* want them to be. Prayer is a means of *relinquishing control* of our plans and asking God to shape our children into the men and women *He* wants them to be.

Isaiah 29:16 tells us, "You turn things upside down, as if the potter were thought to be like the clay! Shall what is formed say to the one who formed it, 'You did not make me'? Can the pot say to the potter, 'You know nothing'?"

God is the Master Potter, and He certainly doesn't need you or me to tell Him how to shape and mold those marvelous jars of clay we call our children. Oh, we'd like to. That's for sure. But God's ultimate goal is for that lump of clay to be fashioned according to His design and for His purposes, not ours. We "train up a child in the way he should go" according to godly principles (Proverbs 22:6a NASB), but God molds the hearts of individuals. "We are the clay, you are the potter," wrote Isaiah. "We are all the work of your hand" (Isaiah 64:8b). I am. You are. Our children are.

Prayer is not a means of *gaining control* over our children, to whip them into shape and make them the men and women *we* want them to be. Prayer is a means of *relinquishing control* of our plans and asking God to shape our children into the men and women *He* wants them to be.

God shapes and molds. We pray and intercede. James 4:3 warns about the danger of praying with wrong motives. "God answers prayer, but He doesn't follow instructions."[3] Check your desire to control and create a "mini me" at the door of the prayer closet, and don't let it in.

As you pray, remember that God already has your child's best interests in mind. Amazingly, He invites you to play a part in the miracle of maturing your child into the adult He created them to be. And as you pray, God aligns your desires with His desires, your thinking with His thinking, and your heart with His heart.

Ezekiel gives us a glimpse into the heart of God regarding prayer. Israel had sinned in every possible way, and her people were doomed for destruction. God said, "I looked for someone among them who would build up the wall and stand before me in the gap on behalf of the land so I would not have to destroy it, but I found no one" (Ezekiel 22:30). God looked for someone to pray, to intercede, to stand in the gap between heaven and earth, but there was no one to be found.

Today God is looking for mothers who will stand in the gap for their children and pray for them to experience the fullness of God's blessing. I'm so glad He has found such a mom in you.

The Battle for Our Children

All we have to do is watch the nightly news, scroll through the latest late-breaking reports, or listen to our kids talk about what they heard on the school bus to know that we are in a battle for the hearts and minds of our children today. Cultural relativism, sexual experimentation, multiple school shootings, unnatural gender confusion, and moral liberalism infest and infect all that God created and called good. Our children trudge through the land mines of evil every day.

Interestingly, Paul referred to prayer in the context of warfare.

> Finally, be strong in the Lord and in his mighty power. Put
> on the full armor of God, so that you can take your stand
> against the devil's schemes. For our struggle is not against
> flesh and blood, but against the rulers, against the authori-
> ties, against the powers of this dark world and against the
> spiritual forces of evil in the heavenly realms. Therefore
> put on the full armor of God, so that when the day of evil
> comes, you may be able to stand your ground, and after you
> have done everything, to stand. Stand firm then, with the
> belt of truth buckled around your waist, with the breastplate
> of righteousness in place, and with your feet fitted with the
> readiness that comes from the gospel of peace. In addition
> to all this, take up the shield of faith, with which you can
> extinguish all the flaming arrows of the evil one. Take the
> helmet of salvation and the sword of the Spirit, which is the
> word of God. And pray in the Spirit on all occasions.… Be
> alert and always keep on praying for all the Lord's people.
> (Ephesians 6:10–18)

A spiritual battle is going on all around us—always has been and
always will be. What began in Genesis 3 continues today. Paul urges us
to be spiritually prepared and physically alert. He emphasized this again
in his second letter to the Corinthians: "Though we live in the world, we
do not wage war as the world does. The weapons we fight with are not
the weapons of the world. On the contrary, they have divine power to
demolish strongholds" (2 Corinthians 10:3–4).

And what are the weapons Paul is referring to? Prayer and God's Word. Look back at Ephesians 6. Only one part of the armor is not defensive but offensive: "the sword of the Spirit, which is the word of God" (v. 17b). How did Jesus win the battle against the devil in the wilderness, recorded in Matthew 4? With Scripture! Every time Satan tempted Jesus to disobey His Father and take control of His own life, Jesus struck down the lies of the enemy with the Word of God. "It is written" was the sword Jesus used to win the war (Matthew 4:4, 6–7, 10). And that is what we will be doing as well. When we pray the Word of God, we pray the will of God. His Word is living and powerful. It is sharper than a double-edged sword (Hebrews 4:12).

As believers, we have authority over the enemy who seeks to harm our children (Luke 10:19). Through prayer, the enemy's plans are intercepted; the principalities and authorities are defeated. Through prayer, the power and provision of God flow into the lives of His people.

God said, "The rain and snow come down from the heavens and stay on the ground to water the earth. They cause the grain to grow, producing seed for the farmer and bread for the hungry. It is the same with my word. I send it out, and it always produces fruit. It will accomplish all I want it to, and it will prosper everywhere I send it" (Isaiah 55:10–11 NLT). And I can assure you that as you pray God's Word, it will always produce fruit and accomplish what God intends.

Pressing Through When You Feel Worn-Out

I want to give you a holy hug right now and let you know there will be days, months, even years when you feel discouraged because of the lack of fruit you see from your prayers. Your prayer might be, "God, throw me a bone! Show me something to let me know my prayers are really making a difference!"

Oh, dear sister, I've been there. What I want to tell you is that God is always working behind the scenes in ways we will never know this side of heaven. Jesus said, "My Father has been working until now [He has never ceased working], and I too am working" (John 5:17 AMP). In another book I wrote, "Our limited vision doesn't allow us to see how God is working behind the questionable scenes in our lives, but we must believe that he is.... The truth is, God is always working, whether we recognize it or not. In fact, it may be precisely in the moments we sense him or understand him the least that he is working the most."[4]

Praying for our children does not mean they won't struggle. Often it is through the struggle that God's does some of His most amazing work! It does mean that we are calling on God to miraculously work in the process. We are petitioning Him for wisdom as we parent, and seeking His presence, power, and protection in the lives of our children.

Every parent will feel discouraged and disheartened when their child makes a decision that we know will lead down a rocky path. However, that rocky path could be the very detour God uses to draw them into a deeper relationship with Him. Don't give up when those boulder-sized struggles litter the way. Keep praying. God is always working.

In the Bible there's a story about a distraught father who had an unruly son with multiple physical and emotional problems. Many people said the boy was possessed by a demon. The dad had tried everything, but the boy continued to demonstrate disturbing actions, such as throwing himself in fire and then in water. That sort of behavior, on top of frequent seizures, rolling on the ground, foaming at the mouth, and an inability to talk, made the dad desperate to find a solution. He even took the boy to some faith healers who were traveling through his hometown. But nothing seemed to work.

Then one day, the father heard Jesus was visiting in his community. He boldly brought the boy to the healer, and with desperation in his voice, cried, "If you can do anything, take pity on us and help us."

And Jesus answered, "'If you can'? Everything is possible for one who believes."

Immediately the boy's father cried out, "I do believe; help me overcome my unbelief!" (Mark 9:22–24).

With that profession, Jesus healed the man's son. (See vv. 14–29 for the full story.)

Oh, how this story stirs my heart. Can't you feel the father's pain? How desperate he must have felt every time the child threw himself into the water or the fire. "Why, son? Why do you do these things?" he must have asked. "I don't understand."

Imagine the humiliation the whispers brought as the family walked down the streets. "That's the Smith family. Have you heard about their son? He's …" The stares, the snickers, the off-color comments. Don't you know there were many days when this dad wanted to give up? Instead, he offers us a beautiful picture of what all parents must do, the ultimate act in parenting: hand our children over to God.

Parenting comes with exhilarating highs and excruciating lows. At times we find ourselves at the end of mental and emotional resources. We feel we have done everything humanly possible and don't know the best action to take with our children. That's exactly where God wants us to be—every day, not depending on our own limited strength and ability but on His limitless power and divine sovereignty. It's when we realize that we will never have all the child-rearing answers and solutions that we discover the importance of giving our children to God. Nineteenth- and early-twentieth-century evangelical minister Samuel D. Gordon, in *Quiet Talks on Prayer*, said, "You can do *more* than pray, *after* you have prayed. But you can *not* do more than pray *until* you have prayed."[5]

Neither you nor I will ever be the perfect parent, but we can be praying parents to a perfect God. Prayer turns an ordinary parent into a powerful force. One of the most magnificent moments in heaven will be when God rolls back the curtain that separates the physical and spiritual realms, and we get to see the connection between our prayers and God's answers. With that said, let me leave you with this poem by Larry Clark:

The Warrior

This morning my thoughts traveled along
To a place in my life where days have since gone
Beholding an image of what I used to be
As visions were stirred and God spoke to me

He showed me a Warrior, a soldier in place
Positioned by Heaven, yet I saw not the face
I watched as The Warrior fought enemies
That came from the darkness with destruction for me

I watched as The Warrior would dry away tears
As all of Heaven's Angels hovered so near
I saw many wounds on The Warrior's face
Yet weapons of warfare were firmly in place

I felt my heart weeping, my eyes held so much
As God let me feel The Warrior's prayer touched
I thought "how familiar" the words that were prayed
The prayers were like lightning that never would fade

I said to God "please, The Warrior's name"
He gave no reply, He chose to refrain
I asked, "Lord, who is broken that they need such
    prayer?"
He showed me an image of myself standing there

Bound by confusion, lost and alone
I felt prayers of The Warrior carry me home
I asked "please show me Lord, this Warrior so true"
I watched and I wept, for Mother, The Warrior was you!

Larry S. Clark[6]

Chapter 2

The Landmarks of Prayer

In this chapter we'll look at the road map and the landmarks for this guide on how to pray for your child from head to toe.

The Mind: What My Child Thinks About

Before children can walk or talk, their brains are being wired by what they see, hear, taste, touch, and experience in their little world—home or otherwise. Amazingly, 90 percent of brain growth happens before kindergarten.[1] Neurological pathways form in the brain that serve as road maps for how someone processes information and forms thoughts. The more our thoughts travel along particular roadways, the deeper the ruts become.

Think of a truck riding down a dirt road ... every day ... several times a day. After a year or so, the ruts in the road become so deep the driver doesn't even have to steer. The wheels just slip right into those ruts and move along.

It's the same way with thoughts. When thoughts play repeatedly in our minds, the ruts become deeper and deeper, and the mental tires just slide into the grooves and move along. In our children's lives (and ours) some of the ruts are good and some are bad; some of them are truth and some are lies. Those ruts are called *neurological pathways*—the paths by which our thoughts move along. That's why the Bible instructs believers, "Do not conform to the pattern of this world, but be transformed by the renewing of your mind" (Romans 12:2a). Once we come to Christ, we begin the process of forming new thought patterns that align with God's truth. But wouldn't it be wonderful if the ruts (neurological pathways) lined up with God's truth in the very beginning!

The Bible has over 160 verses mentioning the mind. This shows us God is very concerned about what happens in a person's thought life. Here are just a few:

> For as he thinks within himself, so he is. (Proverbs 23:7a NASB)

> Set your **mind**s on things above, not on earthly things. (Colossians 3:2)

> Those who live according to the flesh have their **mind**s set on what the flesh desires; but those who live in accordance with the Spirit have their **mind**s set on what the Spirit desires. The **mind** governed by the flesh is death, but the **mind** governed by the Spirit is life and peace." (Romans 8:5–6)

Test me, LORD, and try me, examine my heart and my
mind. (Psalm 26:2)

So you can see why we're starting at the top by praying for the mind.
So many times, we try to change the way our children act. However,
no one can act differently than they think or believe. Godly thinking
produces godly actions. What children think about will ultimately
determine what they are about.

As you pray for your child's mind, you'll be praying for the
thoughts that come to their mind, tumble about in their head, and
affect their actions and emotions. You'll be praying for God to guard
your child's thought life, to keep ungodly thoughts out and wholesome
thoughts in.

The Eyes: What My Child Looks At

I still remember the moment when the nurse placed my newborn son on
my chest, and I looked into those scrunched-up eyes … and he looked
into mine. It was as if he were saying, "Oh, I know you. I recognize your
voice. You're my mommy!"

At birth, babies can only see objects eight to fifteen inches away and
only in black, white, and shades of gray. As the months go by, they begin
to see in color. Babies especially like to fixate on faces. Have you ever
been behind a baby in a buggy at the grocery store checkout? That child
is looking around for someone to make eye contact with, and if you're
that person, that baby will stare you down until you look away. Babies
love looking into someone's eyes. It's as if they are silently asking, *Do you
see me? Do you like me?*

And so it begins, the journey of interpreting the world around them through the portal of their eyes. What we look at affects what we think about.

Studies show that other than sleeping and eating, Americans are likely to watch television more than any other activity.[2] Add to that the internet, video games, social media, and other electronic devices and it's easy to see how screen time affects a child's mind, will, emotions, worldview, and relationships.

As you pray for your child's eyes, you'll be praying for the windows to their soul to be open wide to all God's blessings and handiwork, while the blinds remain closed to anything the world and the enemy would use to distract or destroy. You'll be praying for what your child looks at, chooses not to look at, and processes.

The Ears: Who and What My Child Listens To

All day long children are assailed by noise. From the time they open their eyes in the morning until they close them again at night, children listen to and internalize words, music, nature, and a cacophony of sounds. From the din of discord to the calm of compatibility, what children listen to affects their beliefs about God, about their perception of self, and about the world in general. If children listen to the wrong voices, they will make the wrong choices.

And just like what your child looks at, what they listen to affects thoughts, actions, and emotions. While no one can turn off the world's noise, you can pray your child will lean into what is wholesome and turn away from what is unhealthy both spiritually and emotionally. Just as young Samuel heard the Lord's voice speaking to him in the still of the night, you can pray your child will detect God's voice speaking to their heart.

All through the Bible we read of God speaking to young men and women. He spoke to teenage Mary, adolescent David, and youthful Timothy. And He can speak to your child as well.

As you pray for your child's ears, you'll be praying for what and whom they hear automatically and listen to intentionally—that they will tune in to what is helpful and tune out what is harmful.

The Mouth: Words My Child Speaks

When God created the world, He did so with words. He spoke, and what was not became what is. "By the word of the LORD the heavens were made, their starry host by the breath of his mouth" (Psalm 33:6). God said, "Let there be," and then there was (Genesis 1:3, 6, 14). Amazingly, when He created humans in His own image, He gave us the incredible gift of words. Creative. Powerful. Words.

The Bible tells us, "Death and life are in the power of the tongue" (Proverbs 18:21a NASB). God told the Israelites, "I will do to you the very thing I heard you *say*" (Numbers 14:28b). Jesus said to speak to a mountain, and it would be removed (Mark 11:23). Many great miracles in the Bible occurred because someone spoke. Jesus healed the sick, cast out demons, raised the dead, calmed the storm, and withered a fig tree ... with only the power of His words.

From the very first time my child puckered his cherub lips and formed the word *no*, I knew I was in for a wild ride of the will. Words. They are powerful. As you pray for your child's words, you will be praying that they will learn how to speak kindly and carefully, truthfully and tastefully, respectfully and responsibly, compassionately and courteously, decently and decisively. You will be praying they will not use words cruelly or crudely, hurtfully or hatefully, deceitfully or dishonestly, obscenely or obnoxiously.

Author and marketing guru Roy Williams once said, "Words start wars and end them, create love and choke it, bring us to laughter and joy and tears. Words cause men and women to willingly risk their lives, their fortunes, and their sacred honor. Our world, as we know it, revolves on the power of words."[3]

I must add this here. "Monkey see. Monkey do. Monkey do the same as you." Children are listening to the words their parents speak. If they hear parents using foul or coarse language that complains, ridicules, berates, teases, or lies, then most likely they will do it too. We shouldn't expect otherwise. However, it they hear their parents use words that encourage, honor, respect, praise, compliment, or express gratitude, then most likely they will do the same. So we practice what we pray and model what it means to speak life.

As you are praying for words your child speaks, you'll be praying that God will set a guard over their mouth and keep watch over the door of their lips (Psalm 141:3)—that your child will use the gift of words wisely to build up and not tear down, to bring peace and not dissention.

The Neck: Decisions That Turn My Child's Head

There it was.

Carved in wood.

The evidence could not be denied.

My niece Anna dropped her kids off at school and then went home to clean up a bit. She removed a hairbrush, school papers, and yesterday's jewelry from her dresser. And there it was. She couldn't believe her eyes.

A nail.

And a name.

L-i-l-l-i-a-n … carved into the top of her dresser's walnut surface.

Seven-year-old L-i-l-l-i-a-n didn't even bother to hide the weapon used to commit the crime. The nail lay just where she found it. Right on the dresser by her name.

It was a tough six hours as Anna waited for her forty-four-inch, forty-nine-pound lump of love to get off the school bus. This was not a good day.

"Come with me," Anna said to little Lillian. "I want to show you something."

"What's this about?" Anna asked, pointing to *L-i-l-l-i-a-n* carved into the wood.

Lillian's rosy lower lip quivered, her green eyes filled with tears, and her porcelain face turned autumn red.

"I'm sorry," she whimpered with bowed head.

"What were you thinking?" Anna asked sternly.

"Well," she began, "last night I was waiting for the boys to finish their shower so I could take my turn. I saw the nail and picked it up. At first, when I thought about carving my name on the dresser, my mind said, *No, no, no, don't do it.* But the longer I waited and the longer I thought about it, the *no, no, no, don't do it* turned into *yes, yes, yes, do it.* And I did. I knew it was wrong, but I just had to do it."

Anna got down on her knees and held Lillian's cherubic but very guilty face in her hands. "That's how the devil works," Anna said. "He creeps in when we don't expect it and tells us to do bad things—wrong things; but it is up to us to say no."

"I'm sorry, Mommy," Lillian cried. "I'll never listen to the devil again."

Don't you wish we could all just decide, *I'll never listen to the devil again*, and be done with making bad decisions! Don't you wish our kids could.

But we will always be faced with decisions to choose right and wrong, good and bad, better and best throughout our entire lives … and it begins the moment we take our first breath.

We've looked at your child's mind, eyes, ears, and mouth. Now we get to that vertical connection that turns the head to the left or the right, up or down. This or that. Yes or no. The neck that *turns* the head.

One of the weightiest gifts and responsibilities God gave human-kind at creation was the gift of choice—or free will. While God is sovereign over all the earth, including time and history, He still allows mere humans to make decisions that affect destinies. When it comes to parenting, watching our children make choices will bring us to our knees quicker than any other aspect of being a mom or dad. Whether it's a toddler choosing a toy or a teen selecting a college, making decisions is part of every child's life. Those choices start off small and seemingly insignificant and grow in complexity and consequence. Decisions determine destinies; choices create histories.

What will turn your child's head? Will Jesus be the North Star of their moral compass? Or will they be swayed by the ever-changing mores of a culture that takes what is wrong today and, with a majority vote, makes it right tomorrow? Will they choose to make honoring God the highest priority or default to pleasing self?

As you pray for your child's neck, you'll be praying for the choices they make throughout the day, throughout life, asking God to turn their head *toward* God-honoring decisions and *away from* godless desires.

The Shoulders: Burdens and Worries

I was FaceTiming my niece's four-year-old girl, Harper, who was telling me all about her guinea pig, Skitters. I told her that I'd had a guinea pig named Oscar when I was her same age. "What happened to him?" she asked. "Did he run away, or did he die? Did he go to heaven? Will Skitters go to heaven when he dies?"

I wasn't quite prepared to delve into the inevitable fate of guinea pigs. What I did realize was that Harper was worried. With furrowed brow and tightening tummy, Harper—even at four—was concerned with Skitters's mortality.

You don't have to be an adult with a mortgage, a career, and a family to feel the weight of the world on your shoulders. Children worry. They worry about parents' marital conflict, being abandoned, or becoming sick. They worry about girlfriends and boyfriends, tests and grades, being smaller or larger than their classmates, being accepted or rejected by their peers, and attractions to the opposite sex and friendships with their own sex. New to our current culture is the concern about school violence, sexual molestation, bullying, natural disasters, and pandemics. "Stress among children is estimated to have increased 45% over the past 30 years."[4]

"I feel like I have the weight of my world on my shoulders" is a common lament today. The good news is, Jesus has a solution to that! He said, "Come to me, all you who are weary and burdened [worried and weighed down], and I will give you rest. Take my yoke upon you and learn from me, for I am gentle and humble in heart, and you will find rest for your souls. For my yoke is easy and my burden is light" (Matthew 11:28–30).

And Peter encourages us, "Give all your worries and cares to God, for he cares about you" (1 Peter 5:7 NLT). Isn't that a great reminder! As you pray for your child, I want you to pray this for yourself too!

As you pray for your child's shoulders, you'll be lifting their worries and burdens to the only One able to carry them all, and modeling how to transfer anxiety and apprehension to the One who knows your child best and loves them most.

The Heart: Who and What My Child Loves

Lauren and her husband walked into the doctor's office not sure what to expect. At the nurse's instruction, Lauren slipped off her clothes, put on a grayish-blue hospital gown, and lay down on the examination table. Then the nurse opened the front of the gown, rubbed a cool gel over Lauren's tummy, and began moving a metal wand over the area like an explorer looking for treasure.

After a few moments, a whooshing noise filled the room and a rapid, tiny heartbeat appeared on the screen—150 beats per minute, determined and strong. Suddenly, the couple realized there were not just three people in the room; there were four.

I can't think of many things more exciting than to see and hear a baby's heartbeat for the first time. Amazingly, that swooshing heartbeat begins five to six weeks into pregnancy, and the heart itself is fully developed by the tenth week. And that sound means one thing … there is life.

In the Bible, the word "heart," *lebab* in Old Testament Hebrew and *kardia* in the New Testament Greek, occurs over one thousand times. Most of the time the word doesn't refer to the blood-pumping organ in our chests but represents the seat of our emotional, physical, and intellectual being. It's what shapes our character, words, deeds, and decisions.

However, both the blood-pumping heart in our chests and the decision-making, affection-giving heart of the soul are signs of life!

The Bible instructs us, "Keep your heart with all vigilance, for from it flow the springs of life" (Proverbs 4:23 ESV). "Springs of life" implies that everything we do flows from the heart. The heart is the hidden spring of life that directs the course of our daily choices and lifelong decisions. In the Bible, the heart is the seat of joy (John 16:22), desires (Matthew 5:28), affections (Luke 24:32), perceptions (John 12:40), thoughts (Matthew 9:4), understanding (Matthew 13:15), reasoning (Mark 2:6–8), imagination (Luke 1:51), conscience (Acts 2:37), intentions (Hebrews 4:12), purpose (Acts 11:23), will (Romans 6:17), and faith (Mark 11:23).

Your child's heart is the hub of the wheel into which all the spokes of their life are attached. I've noticed that what we love influences what we become. When someone's heart is right with God, everything else falls into place.

Paul prayed that the Ephesians would be able to "grasp how wide and long and high and deep" the love of Christ was for them (Ephesians 3:17–18). He longed for them to not just know about God and His love for them in their minds but also in their hearts.

As you pray for your child's heart, you'll be praying for what and whom they love, the people they treasure, the possessions they cherish, and the priorities they establish. Also, you'll be praying for a deep understanding of God's love in their heart—the wellspring from which all of life flows.

The Back: Physical and Spiritual Protection

My husband was driving down the highway with my six-year-old son when a car going the opposite direction turned in front of them to pull into a Walmart parking lot. Steve didn't even have time to apply his brakes. Both cars spun before stopping in a mangle of metal and glass. While the cars were destroyed, the drivers and passengers emerged unscathed.

"You were very lucky," the policeman said to six-year-old Steven as he wrote up the report. "No sir," Steven replied. "It wasn't luck. God protected us."

Oh, how my momma's heart swelled when Steve told me of Steven's response. I wondered if another momma was praying for the teenager who was driving the other car.

In Psalm 91:11–12 David wrote, "He will command his angels concerning you to guard you in all your ways; they will lift you up in their hands, so that you will not strike your foot against a stone." But we know the world teems with trouble much greater than hitting our foot against a stone. If we could see what God and His angels protect us from every day, we'd probably be afraid to leave our homes.

The Bible tells us that our "adversary the devil walks about like a roaring lion, seeking whom he may devour" (1 Peter 5:8b NKJV). But it also tells us that "the Spirit who lives in you is greater than the spirit who lives in the world" (1 John 4:4b NLT).

As we've already established in chapter 1, "the weapons we fight with are not the weapons of the world. On the contrary, they have divine power to demolish strongholds" and defeat the enemy's attacks (2 Corinthians 10:4). We pray. God protects.

God is our stronghold in times of trouble (Psalm 18:2), our shield in times of danger (Proverbs 30:5), and our fortress in times of attack

(Psalm 91:1–2). He protects us not only in the physical realm, which we can see, but also in the spiritual realm against forces we can't see (2 Corinthians 10:3–4). A spiritual battle rages around your child as the devil attempts to kill, steal, and destroy (John 10:10). He sets traps in the path of God's people, hoping to catch them unaware and ill prepared. Oh, how he despises praying mammas who thwart his plans.

As I mentioned earlier, Paul's letter to the Ephesians instructs us to "put on the full armor of God" (Ephesians 6:11a). But his detailed description of the spiritual armor does not point to any item protecting the back. That's where we come in ... covering the backs of our children with prayer.

As you pray for your child's back, you'll be praying for protection in the physical and spiritual realms with the assurance that no weapon turned against them will succeed (Isaiah 54:17 NLT).

The Arms: Health and Strength

She wasn't a weight lifter, nor was she on the girl's wrestling team, but the moment I met Katie Signaigo, I knew that she was amazingly strong. Katie had lost her leg due to cancer when she was eleven, and though it was heartbreaking and gut-wrenching at the time, I listened to this eighteen-year-old young woman tell of how God had made her stronger through the struggle. And one year later, I applauded as she walked the runway with her prosthetic leg in the Miss University of Central Arkansas pageant ... and won. She went on to compete in Miss Arkansas and appeared on the Oprah Winfrey show. And today, this momma of three still amazes me.

How do *you* determine how strong someone is? Many would say it is by how much weight a person can lift. Some would argue it is how much weight a body can carry. Others would say strength is determined by how long someone can endure or sustain an action. Webster defines *strength* as "the capacity to exert force, resist attack, or resist strain, stress, etc."[5]

In the Bible, God's strength is symbolized by His arm. The psalmist wrote, "The strong right arm of the LORD is raised in triumph. The strong right arm of the LORD has done glorious things!" (Psalm 118:16 NLT). "Powerful is your arm!" (Psalm 89:13a NLT). Moses reminded the Israelites: "Remember that you were slaves in Egypt and that the LORD your God brought you out of there with a mighty hand and an outstretched arm" (Deuteronomy 5:15a). The Israelites praised God, "who sent his glorious arm of power to be at Moses' right hand" (Isaiah 63:12a).

In contrast to our infinitely powerful God, all children at one time or another will struggle with feelings of weakness, whether it's dealing with disappointment or devastating news, saying no when peers are saying yes, pressing on when emotions say to give up, or holding back when tempted to give in. We can pray that our children will be strong and courageous in a world of weakness and carnal cravings.

Paul tells us the secret to his success: "When I am weak, then I am strong" (2 Corinthians 12:10b) and "I can do all this through him who gives me strength" (Philippians 4:13). Human weakness becomes the backdrop for God's strength to shine. That's what we want our kids to learn.

As we come to this landmark of prayer, your child's arms, we'll borrow from the biblical symbolism and pray for our child's health and strength. But it's not heavy lifting that will make your child spiritually and emotionally strong. True strength comes when they allow their life to become a conduit through which God's strength flows.

As you pray for your child's arms, you'll be praying that they will not depend on their own strength but, instead, will rely on God's strength.

You'll be praying for strength of character, courage, and purpose to be all God has fashioned them to be. You will be praying that God will make them physically, emotionally, and spiritually strong.

The Hands: Gifts and Talents

"What do you want to be when you grow up?" I asked a roomful of first graders. "A fireman!" "A teacher!" "The president!" "A veterinarian!" "A professional basketball player!" "A princess!" "Beautiful!" (Not kidding.) "A truck driver!"

It doesn't take long for a child to start to think about what kind of job they want to have when they're all grown up. Of course, those desires change multiple times from first grade to middle school to high school. It even changes after! My son changed his mind with his shoe size. Career choices are important no matter what that career it is.

Right from the start, God gave Adam and Eve a job to do and a purpose to fulfill. "Be fruitful and increase in number; fill the earth and subdue it. Rule over the fish in the sea and the birds in the sky and over every living creature that moves on the ground" (Genesis 1:28). After Adam and Eve disobeyed God, their work became difficult. And even though there are thorns and thistles in every job, men and women are still called to work. I'm not just talking about a career or working at home. I'm talking about work period. Schoolwork, homework, house-work, yardwork, artwork.

As parents, we look for gifts and talents in our children. The Bible says, "Train up a child in the way *he* should go" (Proverbs 22:6a NASB)—note that specific *he* or *she*. Scripture also lets us know that everyone has certain God-given gifts, talents, and abilities. David had a knack for slinging rocks. Bezalel was good at working with gold and silver. Joseph was gifted at organization and administration. Lydia was a great seamstress. Abigail surprised everyone with her negotiation skills.

I love what Hebrews 11:23 says about Moses's parents: "By faith Moses' parents hid him for three months after he was born, because they saw he was no ordinary child." What mother hasn't thought the same about her own?

As you pray for your child's hands, you'll be praying that they will discover their unique giftings, develop their God-given potential, discern their purpose, and desire to glorify God in all their endeavors (1 Corinthians 10:31).

The Ring Finger: Future Spouse

Steven was in the sixth grade when he and I were sitting at the kitchen table, eating our peanut butter and jelly sandwiches. At one point he sheepishly looked up and said, "Mom, you know Rosemary in my class? I think I'd like to get her a little something for her birthday." And so it began! A new kind of flutter in a little boy's heart.

From the time Steven was born, Steve and I prayed for his future spouse. I had seen bad marriages. I had seen good marriages. Because I had grown up in a difficult home environment, when I was a teenager, I decided that I would not marry anyone unless he loved Jesus more than he loved me. Even my own father told me that my standards were too high, and I needed to let boys be boys. I knew exactly what Dad meant, and I wanted no part of that kind of a forever relationship. Then one day, God answered my prayer exceedingly abundantly more than I could have ever asked or imagined (Ephesians 3:20 NASB). I met Steve Jaynes at a college Bible study and knew that I knew that I knew.

Choosing a spouse is one of the most important decisions a person can make, second only to accepting Jesus as Savior and Lord. However, not everyone is meant to be married. The apostle Paul felt singleness was a blessing (1 Corinthians 7:7). As far as we know, neither Mary nor Martha was married but lived with their brother, Lazarus (Luke 10:38–39; John 11:1). We never want our adult children to feel like they are incomplete if they are not married or that their identity is wrapped up in having a spouse. True contentment and fulfillment can only be found in a relationship with Christ.

However, when our children are growing up, we don't know what God has in store in the marriage department. So in this prayer journey, we are going to pray as if our children will one day find that special someone and say, "I do." When you pray for your child's future spouse, you'll be praying that your child's mate will come to know Christ at an early age, grow spiritually mature and emotionally strong, and develop into the better half of the eventual whole.

The Side: Influential Relationships

My childhood home was a hornet's nest of contention, and I lived my first decade in abject fear. My parents fought verbally and physically in front of me, and many nights I hid in the closet with my hands over my ears. I saw things a child should never see and heard words a child should never hear. Heading into my tween years, I was on my way to making bad choices with questionable friends. I was looking for anyone who would give me a hint of approval.

But when I was twelve, I started a new friendship with a little redheaded girl in my neighborhood. I loved being in Wanda's home. Something was different there. Her parents loved each other, and they

Your child faces
decisions throughout
the day that
determine whether
they will walk in
tandem with Jesus
or in sync with the
world. Steps become
a lifestyle; a lifestyle
becomes a legacy.

loved their girls. And while I didn't understand all the reasons that family was so different from mine, I knew it had something to do with Jesus. Through this family, I came to know Jesus as my Savior. And within six years of my decision to follow Christ, both of my parents became Christians as well. Wanda and I are friends to this day.

Friends. The people we choose to walk side by side with in relationship affects our choices, character, and conduct for good or bad. The Bible warns us, "Bad company corrupts good character" (1 Corinthians 15:33b). It also tells us that those who walk with wise people become wise themselves (Proverbs 13:20).

When Jesus walked the earth in human flesh, He did so in the context of relationships. He could have accomplished God's redemptive plan all by Himself. But He chose to live in relationship with others to carry out the miracles, messages, and ministry of those three and a half years. His friends, family, and followers often made His life on earth more difficult. He lived in a family that often did not understand Him (Mark 3:20–21, 31–34), a community that often did not accept Him (Mark 6:1–6), and with a bunch of men who often did not believe Him (Matthew 16:21–23).

Jesus ministered to the multitudes, but He also had a close relationship with seventy-two followers, a closer relationship with a group of twelve, and a heart-to-heart connection with three: Peter, James, and John. Even then, it was His heavenly Father with whom Jesus communed on the most intimate level in moment-by-moment abiding.

Father, mother, sisters, brothers, aunts, uncles, sons, daughters, friends, bosses, employees, coworkers, neighbors, and the list goes on. Your child is surrounded by relationships that can affect them for good or for bad. But I daresay, parents and peers are the most impactful.

We are all sponges, soaking up the personas of those with whom we walk side by side. The people with whom your child spends time affect their attitudes, character, behavior, speech, and outlook on life. Relationships are the change agents God uses to sand away the rough edges of the flesh and shore up the weak places of the soul. They can be the voices on the sidelines cheering them on and willing them to get back up when they fall.

As you pray for your child's side, you'll be praying for their relationships, friendships, and partnerships—the people who influence their actions, attitudes, character, and future.

Sexuality: Sexual Purity and Identity

Everywhere we turn these days we're hit with a barrage of sexual images attacking our senses. Television, movies, the internet, display windows, music lyrics, and more. By the time a teen graduates from high school, he or she will have seen no fewer than fourteen thousand depictions of and references to sex on television per year.[6]

Remaining sexually pure until marriage may seem like an antiquated and unrealistic idea in a culture that views hookup sex as normal and expected. Have we gone so far as to even think it is impossible for our children to show restraint? I don't think so, but it won't be easy.

It's not that sex is a bad thing. Quite the opposite. As God said after He created all the intricacies in man and woman to make sexual intimacy possible, "It is good, very good" (see Genesis 1:31). Scripture shows us that sex is not an evil that marriage permits but a gift that marriage protects.

I believe the problem is not that our culture focuses on sex too much but that it values sex too little. Sex is meant to be so much more than a physical act of hormonal urges. Sex was created to be a sacred union between a husband and wife, designed by a holy, ingenious, and immensely generous God. As our children get old enough to understand, it's our responsibility to let them know that God intended sex to be a gift to be enjoyed in the safe boundaries of marriage. We never want them to think sex is bad or dirty but a beautiful gift that is worth unwrapping at the right time.

When talking to our children about sex, we need to make sure they understand that God isn't a spoilsport who wants to keep people from having fun, but an ingenious Creator who wants husbands and wives to experience the best intimacy possible. Many in our culture have traded in the invaluable treasure of marital lovemaking for dime-store hookup sex. That's certainly what is portrayed on television and on the video screen. But it doesn't have to be this way. The Bible boldly paints a beautiful, contrasting picture of sexual intimacy as it could be if we pursue love the way God purposed it to be from the beginning.

One day, while I was writing the book *Lovestruck: God's Design for Romance, Marriage, and Sexual Intimacy from the Song of Solomon*, I was sitting beside a twenty-three-year-old young man in an airplane. We bantered back and forth about where we were from and what we did back home. The conversation eventually swung around to my work as a writer.

"What are you working on now?" he asked.

Heat crept up my neck as I cautiously replied, "I'm writing a book on marriage and sex based on the Song of Solomon in the Bible."

Without batting an eye, he replied, "I'm so glad you're doing that. My generation is so mixed up when it comes to sex. They hook up with people they barely know. By the time they get married, they've slept with so many different people that sex has lost its specialness. We need to know how to do it the right way."

I just wanted to give him a hug.

So let's pray, pray, pray.

Another issue that we must tackle in the prayer closet is gender identity. The Bible says that when God created mankind, "male and female he created them" (Genesis 1:27b). He didn't make a mistake or leave something out or add something extra in the mix when He knitted your child together in the womb. So we are going to pray that our children will embrace and celebrate the genders God fashioned and formed their bodies to be.

As you pray for your child's sexual purity and identity, you'll be praying against promiscuity and for restraint. You'll also be praying that they embrace and celebrate the gender of their birth.

The Legs: Stand for Godly Principles

When I was in grade school, I learned that Pluto was the ninth planet in our solar system. In 2006 scientists said, "Oops, it's not really a planet after all." It was downgraded to "dwarf planet" status and bumped off the list of nine planets that revolve around our sun. I envisioned thousands of school children plucking the brownish-orange orb from their science project displays. Just another truth that wasn't true after all.

In our culture ideas and ideals that were supposedly true yesterday are declared false today. What's right today may be wrong tomorrow, and what's illegal today may be legal tomorrow. Modern man echoes Pilate's words to Jesus, "What is truth?" (John 18:38a).

We live in a world where cultural relativism is embraced, a culture that says all points of view are equally valid and all truth is relative to the individual. People say things like, "That may be true for you, but that doesn't mean it is true for me." The problem with those words is that if truth can change depending on perspective, place, or time, then it is not true at all. This mindset mirrors that of the Israelites during the time of the Judges: "Everyone did what was right in his own eyes" (Judges 17:6; 21:25 NASB).

But as God has shown us time and time again, truth is an *exclusive* reality, not an elusive myth. There is a truth that transcends culture and individual inclinations. And that truth is Jesus Christ.

Jesus said, "I am the way and the truth and the life" (John 14:6a). "The Word [Jesus] became flesh and made his dwelling among us. We have seen his glory, the glory of the one and only Son, who came from the Father, full of grace and truth" (1:14). Jesus repeatedly started His teachings with the words "I tell you the truth" (NLT) or "Very truly I tell you" (NIV) (5:19, 24–25; 6:26, 32, 53). He is the truth and the source of truth.

So what does all this have to do with praying for the landmark of your child's legs? Everything. Your child needs to *stand* on the truth. All else is shifting sand. If they do not stand on the truth, the world becomes a confusing place. The undertow of uncertainty can pull them out to sea with a riptide of questions and the shifting tides of change. As God told the Israelites, "If you do not stand firm in your faith, you will not stand at all" (Isaiah 7:9b).

And that is a message for all of us. If we do not *stand* on the truth, then we will not *stand* at all. We will be tossed back and forth like a spineless rag doll by a childlike world that pitches a fit to get its own way.

As you pray for your child's legs, you'll be praying that they will stand firm in faith in a wishy-washy world. You'll be praying that they will stand on the unchanging, infallible truth of God.

The Knees: Relationship with God

Steven was four when he came to me one morning with some matter-of-fact news. "Mommy, I asked Jesus to come into my heart last night."

"You did?" I replied with a smile. "So what happened?"

"He did."

And off he scampered to play with a cousin. We were on a family vacation when Steven nonchalantly revealed his story. I told my husband, Steve, and we just decided to let it sit for a while.

Later that day, Steven told his older cousin the same news with a few more details.

"Last night I got up from my bed and looked out the window at the sky. Then I said, 'Jesus, I want You to come into my heart.' And He did."

Who was I to doubt the authenticity of my little towheaded boy's salvation experience? Jesus said, "Let the little children come to me, and do not hinder them, for the kingdom of heaven belongs to such as these" (Matthew 19:14).

Steven came to Jesus with what he knew, what he had heard. *If you ask Jesus to come into your heart, He will.*

That was the beginning of Steven's journey to the heart of God. Through the years he continued to learn and grow with two steps forward and one step back. When he was twelve, with more knowledge about what it meant to be a Christ follower, he asked to be baptized by a pastor friend in a lake not too far from our home. My husband, who was sprinkled as a baby, decided to be baptized along with him.

It was a wonderful day.

But that was not the end. I didn't wipe my hands and think, *Okay, now I can check that off my list.* No, my prayers for Steven's spiritual maturity were just beginning.

The Christian journey is a lifelong process with periods of rhapsody and apathy, involvement and indifference, passion and disinterest, advancement and decline, questioning and certainty. As mothers, we continue to pray for our children's spiritual growth for as long as we have breath.

Our children's relationship with Jesus is the most important aspect of their lives—everything else pales in comparison. Nothing is more important; everything else is a reflection of it. Their salvation affects not only where they will spend eternity but also how they will handle adversity in the here and now.

As you pray for your child's knees, you'll be praying for them to accept Jesus as Lord and Savior and to continue to grow and mature spiritually. You'll be praying that they will humbly kneel in submission to God, in worship of God, and in communion with God. You'll be praying that their relationship with Jesus will become and remain the most important relationship in all of life.

The Feet: The Path My Child Takes

As soon as our children learn how to walk, we hold their hands to keep them out of harm's way. At first, we hold both of a toddler's hands to keep them from falling over. Then we hold one hand to keep them from wandering away. But eventually, we must let go of that hand and pray they will take hold of God's hand to stay on the right path.

The Christian life is often referred to as our spiritual walk. "Walk by faith, not by sight," Paul encouraged the Corinthian church (2 Corinthians 5:7 NASB). The New International Version translates this same verse, "We live by faith, not by sight."

Paul wrote to the Galatians, "I say then: Walk in the Spirit, and you shall not fulfill the lust of the flesh.... If we live in the Spirit, let us also walk in the Spirit" (Galatians 5:16, 25 NKJV). Again, the New International Version translates these same words: "So I say, walk by the Spirit, and you will not gratify the desires of the flesh.... Since we live by the Spirit, let us keep in step with the Spirit." I love the idea of *keeping in step* with the Holy Spirit. What a wonderful way to live: walking in step and keeping time with the Holy Spirit's pace.

Your child faces decisions throughout the day that determine whether they will walk in tandem with Jesus or in sync with the world. Steps become a lifestyle; a lifestyle becomes a legacy.

So as you come to this final landmark of prayer—your child's feet— you'll be praying for where their feet take them on the journey of life, what paths they choose along the way, and how they will keep in step with God.

Chapter 3

How to Use This Book

I find that many women, including me, are directionally challenged. I need landmarks. Don't tell me to go east or west, north or south. Give me a landmark. Turn right at the red school building. Turn left at the fire station. Look for the teal-colored house around the bend. Those are directions I can follow.

Maybe that's why I love the fact that Jesus taught His disciples to pray using landmarks. When one of His disciples asked, "Lord, teach us to pray" (Luke 11:1b NKJV), Jesus responded:

In this manner, therefore, pray:

Our Father in heaven,
Hallowed be Your name.
Your kingdom come.
Your will be done
On earth as it is in heaven.
Give us this day our daily bread.
And forgive us our debts,

As we forgive our debtors.

And do not lead us into temptation,

But deliver us from the evil one.

For Yours is the kingdom and the power and the glory

    forever. Amen. (Matthew 6:9–13 NKJV)

Jesus was not instructing the disciples on how to pray a rote prayer. He was giving them a *pattern* for prayer—landmarks: Acknowledge God's fatherhood, holiness, and sovereignty. Ask for His will to be done, your needs to be met, and your sins to be forgiven. Ask for deliverance from temptation and protection from evil. Acknowledge God's rule, reign, power, and glory.

In a similar way, *Praying for Your Child from Head to Toe* will give you landmarks to guide your prayers. This is not a magic formula or a pattern for rote prayer. It is simply a guide for pursuing a more consistent and effective prayer life.

Let's be honest. God's ways are not our ways, and sometimes we don't know what to pray for our child. But we can rest assured that when we pray the *Word of God*, we pray the *will of God*. What a relief!

As we've already seen, when Paul instructed us to put on the armor of God, there was only one weapon. Every other piece—the figurative helmet, breastplate, belt, shield, and shoes—was defensive, intended for protection from the evil one. The sword of the Spirit, which is defined as the Word of God, is the only offensive weapon listed in the whole outfit.

After Paul instructed us to take up the sword of the Spirit, he followed with this: "And pray in the Spirit on all occasions" (Ephesians 6:18a). When you combine the Word of God with Spirit-empowered prayer, you are armed and dangerous against the power of the enemy. You have "divine power to demolish strongholds" (2 Corinthians 10:4b).

In the Greek, the original language of the New Testament, the word translated as "power" is *dunamis*; it speaks of "potential power" and "actual power." It is where we get our English word *dynamite*. God has handed you two powerful sticks of "dynamite" as you intercede for your child: His Word and your prayer. As you strap these two sticks together and ignite the fuse with faith, you will see the power of God act on your behalf and your child's behalf as never before.

As we pray, we will pray to the Father, in the name of Jesus, through the power of the Holy Spirit. The Bible tells us that we have access to the Father through the Son (Ephesians 2:18). "In Jesus' name" is not simply a salutation to a Christian's prayer; it is the source of authority for a believer's prayer. When we pray in Jesus' name, we're admitting that we don't come before God because we are credible or worthy in our own right but credible and worthy because of Jesus' sacrifice for our sins that allows us to approach the holy God—because of grace.

Jesus said to his disciples, "All authority in heaven and on earth has been given to me" (Matthew 28:18). When we pray in Jesus' name, our authority flows from His. However, that authority only goes as far as His will. That's why we are praying Scripture.

Oh sister, there is power in the name of Jesus! He said, "I will do whatever you ask *in my name*, so that the Father may be glorified in the Son (John 14:13). What a gift the Father has given that we can call on that name above every other name.

In part 2 we begin to pray. I have provided a thirty-day guide for interceding for your child from head to toe. Each day you'll find a

Scripture for each landmark and a prayer that incorporates that passage. The verses are from the New International Version unless otherwise marked. It should take approximately five to seven minutes to cover your child daily in powerfully effective, Bible-based prayer. I can't think of a better investment of time!

Many of the prayers are written as if your child were already a Christian; however, I know that some have not made a decision to follow Christ yet. In this case, we will be praying by faith, calling "into being things that were not" (Romans 4:17b).

> The purpose of prayer is to release God's power on earth as it is in heaven.

One way to use the book is to correspond the days of prayer with the dates of the months. For example, on the first day of the month, pray day one; on the second day of the month, pray day two; and so on. If you miss a day, just stay on track with your calendar; then begin again the following month. Of course, you can also simply pray straight through without connecting the days of prayer with the dates on the calendar.

Another way to use this book is to ignore the days altogether. You might be praying along and come to a prayer on a certain day that you need to settle in on and really dig your knees into. No worries. Just camp out there on that one prayer. Don't worry about completing all the prayers every day. If you need to do only a few per day, then that is great too!

If you're like me, you will want to use this book time and time again. You might even want to gather a few girlfriends to form a Praying Moms group and pray for your children together. Jesus said, "Truly I tell you that if two of you on earth *agree* about anything they ask for, it will be done for them by my Father in heaven" (Matthew 18:19). The Greek word for "agree" is *symphōneō*, which means "to sound together, to be in accord, primarily of musical instruments."[1] What a beautiful symphony wafts to the heavenlies when sisters in Christ join in harmonious prayer offered up to God!

No matter which way you choose to use this prayer guide, I know you and your child or children will be blessed "exceedingly abundantly above all that we ask or think" (Ephesians 3:20 NKJV)!

The prophet Isaiah wrote this about God: "Since ancient times no one has heard, no ear has perceived, no eye has seen any God besides you, who acts on behalf of those who wait for him" (Isaiah 64:4). I can't wait to see how God is going to act on your behalf as you lift up your child in prayer.

• • •

Now that we've covered the landmarks of prayer and discussed how to use this book, let's begin the exciting adventure of praying for your child from head to toe. James wrote, "When a believing person prays, great things happen" (James 5:16b NCV). I am so excited just thinking about the great things that are going to happen in your child's life because their mamma prayed.

Part 2

Thirty Days of Praying for Your Child from Head to Toe

Day 1

The Mind: What My Child Thinks About

Jesus replied: "Love the Lord your God with all your heart and with all your soul and with all your mind." (Matthew 22:37)

Heavenly Father, I pray my child will love You completely—with heart, soul, and mind. I pray intellectual knowledge of You will lead to an emotional affection for You.

The Eyes: What My Child Looks At

Turn my eyes from worthless things, and give me life through your word. (Psalm 119:37 NLT)

I pray my child will turn their eyes away from worthless things. I pray they will divert their eyes away from anything or anyone that would cause them to stumble, trip, or fall in thoughts or actions.

The Ears: Who and What My Child Listens To

My children, listen when your father corrects you. Pay attention and learn good judgment, for I am giving you good guidance. Don't turn away from my instructions. For I, too, was once my father's son, tenderly loved as my mother's only child. My father taught me, "Take my words to heart. Follow my commands, and you will live." (Proverbs 4:1–4 NLT)

I pray my child will listen to their parents' instruction, paying attention to what we say and learning good judgment. I pray they will take our words to heart, follow our instruction, and experience a long and productive life.

The Mouth: Words My Child Speaks

Each of you must put off falsehood and speak truthfully to your neighbor, for we are all members of one body. (Ephesians 4:25)

I pray my child will always tell the truth. I pray they will not stretch the truth, tell a half-truth, distort the truth, misrepresent the truth, or embellish the truth.

The Neck: Decisions That Turn My Child's Head

My child, listen to me and do as I say, and you will have a long, good life. I will teach you wisdom's ways and lead you in straight paths. When you walk, you won't be held back; when you run, you won't stumble. Take hold of my instructions; don't let them go. Guard them, for they are the key to life. (Proverbs 4:10–13 NLT)

I pray my child will pay attention to godly instruction and learn good judgment, following wise counsel so that they will have a long, good life. I pray my child will make wise decisions that lead to straight paths so they will move forward and not backward, run and not fall.

The Shoulders: Burdens and Worries

> Is anything too hard for the LORD? (Genesis 18:14a)

No matter what my child must go through today, help them not to worry but believe that nothing is too hard for You.

The Heart: Who and What My Child Loves

> You shall love the LORD your God with all your heart and with all your soul and with all your might. (Deuteronomy 6:5 ESV)

I pray my child will love You will all their heart, soul, and might. May everything and everyone else be a distant second compared to loving You.

The Back: Physical and Spiritual Protection

> The LORD your God moves around in your camp to protect you and to defeat your enemies. (Deuteronomy 23:14a NLT)

Almighty God, I ask that You move about in my child's camp—home, school, and everywhere in between. Protect and deliver them from anyone who would seek to do harm physically, mentally, emotionally, or spiritually.

The Arms: Health and Strength

There the child grew up healthy and strong. He was filled
with wisdom, and God's favor was on him. (Luke 2:40 NLT)

I pray my child will grow up healthy, strong, and filled with wisdom. I
pray that Your favor will rest on them.

Decisions determine destinies; choices create histories.

The Hands: Gifts and Talents

Bless all his skills, LORD, and be pleased with the work of
his hands. (Deuteronomy 33:11a)

Dear Lord, bless my child's skills and be pleased with the work of their
hands. Thank You for giving my child gifts and talents. I pray that as
they continue to grow and mature, they will recognize and exercise the
gifts and talents You have given.

The Ring Finger: Future Spouse

> The LORD God said, "It is not good for the man to be alone. I will make a helper suitable for him." ... That is why a man leaves his father and mother and is united to his wife, and they become one flesh. (Genesis 2:18, 24)

Heavenly Father, besides knowing Jesus as Savior, my child's choice of a spouse is among the most important decisions they will ever make. I pray, even now, that my child and their future spouse will become one in every sense of the word. As a lock is to a key, I pray they will live and move as one. Prepare my child's future spouse to be a godly person who will hold fast to the mate You have chosen for them.

The Side: Influential Relationships

> Honor your father and your mother, as the LORD your God has commanded you, so that you may live long and that it may go well with you in the land the LORD your God is giving you. (Deuteronomy 5:16)

I pray my child will honor their parents, as the Lord God has commanded, so that they may live a long life that goes well. I pray my child will show respect even when angry, follow our rules even when they don't make sense, and value our relationship even when we don't agree.

Sexuality: Sexual Purity and Identity

> The thief comes only to steal and kill and destroy; I have come that they may have life, and have it to the full. (John 10:10)

Thank You, Jesus, that You came to give us life to the full and that includes the gift of marital intimacy. I pray against the wiles of the enemy, who comes to steal, kill, and destroy what you have created for marital union and communion. I pray my child will remain pure until marriage and one day experience sex the way You intended: fully and free, without guilt or remorse.

The Legs: Stand for Godly Principles

> Moses told the people, "Don't be afraid. Just stand still and watch the LORD rescue you today.... The LORD himself will fight for you. Just stay calm." (Exodus 14:13–14 NLT)

Lord, I know there were children among the Israelites crossing the Red Sea. Just as Moses spoke to them, may my child not be afraid when faced with seemingly impossible obstacles that block the path ahead. Just as the Israelites stood firm and stood still to witness Your deliverance and rescue, may my child receive the courage to stand firm and stand still to witness Your deliverance in their life. Help my child not worry or fret but stay calm in the knowledge of Your protection and provision.

The Knees: Relationship with God

> Believe on the Lord Jesus Christ, and you will be saved, you and your household. (Acts 16:31 NKJV)

Lord, this is the most important prayer I can pray for my child. I pray they will believe on the Lord Jesus Christ and be saved. As part of my household, I claim this promise for my child.

The Feet: The Path My Child Takes

> Your word is a lamp to my feet and a light to my path.
> (Psalm 119:105 NKJV)

Finally, I pray Your Word will always be a lamp to my child's feet and a light for their path. May Scripture be the beacon that directs my child's feet away from harm and toward the haven of Your will. I pray all this in Jesus' name, amen.

Day 2

The Mind: What My Child Thinks About

Finally, brothers and sisters, whatever is true, whatever is noble, whatever is right, whatever is pure, whatever is lovely, whatever is admirable—if anything is excellent or praiseworthy—think about such things. (Philippians 4:8)

Father God, I pray my child will fill their mind with whatever is true and not false, whatever is right and not wrong, whatever is pure and not crude, whatever is lovely and not loathsome, whatever is admirable and not despicable. I pray they won't dwell on the negatives of this world but on the positives of Your promises.

The Eyes: What My Child Looks At

Since the creation of the world God's invisible qualities— his eternal power and divine nature—have been clearly seen, being understood from what has been made, so that people are without excuse. (Romans 1:20)

I pray my child will see Your invisible qualities, Your eternal power, and Your divine nature through the universe You have made. I pray they will not miss the splendor of Your creation but see Your glory through the works of Your hand. From the tallest tree to the smallest insect, open their eyes to marvel at Your handiwork.

The Ears: Who and What My Child Listens To

> [Jesus said,] Pay close attention to what you hear. The closer you listen, the more understanding you will be given—and you will receive even more. (Mark 4:24 NLT)

I pray my child will pay close attention to what they hear about godly living and godly principles, knowing that the closer they listen, the more understanding they will receive.

The Mouth: Words My Child Speaks

> May these words of my mouth and this meditation of my heart be *pleasing* in your sight, LORD, my Rock and my Redeemer. (Psalm 19:14)

I pray the words of my child's mouth and the meditation of their heart will be pleasing in Your sight, Lord, our Rock and Redeemer. I pray their words will be acceptable, agreeable, and honorable to You.

The Neck: Decisions That Turn My Child's Head

> Flee youthful passions and pursue righteousness, faith, love, and peace, along with those who call on the Lord from a pure heart. (2 Timothy 2:22 ESV)

As my child makes decisions to do or not to do, to say or not to say, to be or not to be, I pray they will choose Your ways and not the world's ways. I pray they flee youthful passions regardless of what their friends are doing and pursue righteousness, faith, love, and peace, along with others who call on the Lord from a pure heart.

The Shoulders: Burdens and Worries

> I trust in your unfailing love; my heart rejoices in your salvation. I will sing the LORD's praise, for he has been good to me. (Psalm 13:5–6)

I pray my child will not worry or fret about the future but trust in Your unfailing love. I pray they will remember all the times You have been good to them and trust You will continue to be gracious in the future.

The Heart: Who and What My Child Loves

> Jesus replied: "'Love the Lord your God with all your heart and with all your soul and with all your mind." (Matthew 22:37)

I pray my child will love You with all their heart, soul, and mind. Help them to recognize anyone or anything that they love more than You, and give them the wisdom and will to move that thing or person to the proper position. May they love You above all else.

The Back: Physical and Spiritual Protection

> The LORD who rescued me from the paw of the lion and the paw of the bear will rescue me from the hand of this Philistine. (1 Samuel 17:37a)

Almighty Lord, just as You protected David from the paw of the lion, the paw of the bear, and the sword of the giant, I pray You will protect my child from anything or anyone who would seek to do them harm. Help my child to not be afraid of those who appear bigger, stronger, or more powerful but be confident in Your all-encompassing protection and all-sufficient power to save.

The Arms: Health and Strength

> The LORD is my strength and my song, and he has become my salvation. (Exodus 15:2a ESV)

I pray You will be my child's strength and song. Give them the strength to fulfill Your purpose today and every day. Give them strength for every struggle and the victory song for every battle.

The Hands: Gifts and Talents

> Whatever your hand finds to do, do it with all your might. (Ecclesiastes 9:10a)

Whatever my child sets out to do, I pray they will do it with all their might—enthusiastically and excellently.

The Ring Finger: Future Spouse

> You have been taught the holy Scriptures from childhood, and they have given you the wisdom to receive the salvation that comes by trusting in Christ Jesus. (2 Timothy 3:15 NLT)

Lord, I pray my child's future spouse will be taught the Scriptures from childhood. I pray this person we have yet to meet will accept Jesus as Lord and Savior at an early age and continue to grow and mature in the faith. If my child's future spouse's parents do not know Christ, I pray You will send someone to share the gospel with them and that they will give their lives to You.

The Side: Influential Relationships

> Walk with the wise and become wise; associate with fools
> and get in trouble. (Proverbs 13:20 NLT)

I pray my child will form godly friendships with wise people and become wise. I pray they will flee ungodly relationships with foolish people who might lead them in the wrong direction.

Sexuality: Sexual Purity and Identity

> Be strong and courageous, all you who put your hope in
> the LORD! (Psalm 31:24 NLT)

When peer pressure pushes my child toward sexual promiscuity or experimentation, I pray You will give them the power to stand strong and the courage to resist temptation. Help my child equate the word *no* with being bold and brave.

The Legs: Stand for Godly Principles

> The priests who carried the ark of the covenant of the
> LORD stopped in the middle of the Jordan and stood on

dry ground, while all Israel passed by until the whole nation
had completed the crossing on dry ground. (Joshua 3:17)

Give my child the faith to stand firm in the center of Your will, fully
expecting You to perform miracles, wonders, and mighty acts on their
behalf.

The Knees: Relationship with God

Behold, I stand at the door and knock. If anyone hears
my voice and opens the door, I will come in to him and
eat with him, and he with me. (Revelation 3:20 ESV)

Thank You, Jesus, for knocking on the door of my child's heart. Help
them hear Your voice and open the door right away.

The Feet: The Path My Child Takes

Mark out a straight path for your feet; stay on the safe
path. Don't get sidetracked; keep your feet from following evil. (Proverbs 4:26–27 NLT)

Finally, I pray You will mark out a straight path for my child's feet—
setting them securely on the safe path. Help them to not get sidetracked
by the world's enticements that would lead them toward evil pursuits. I
pray all this in Jesus' name, amen.

Day 3

The Mind: What My Child Thinks About

You keep him in perfect peace whose mind is stayed on you, because he trusts in you. (Isaiah 26:3 ESV)

Dear Lord, I pray my child's mind will stay on You today and be at peace. I pray their thoughts won't be tangled up in troubles but calm in holy confidence. Help them trust that You are in control and have their best interest at heart.

The Eyes: What My Child Looks At

When the woman saw that the fruit of the tree was good for food and pleasing to the eye, and also desirable for gaining wisdom, she took some and ate it. She also gave some to her husband, who was with her, and he ate it. (Genesis 3:6)

I pray my child will not be tempted to sin by what is pleasing to the eye but will be strong to resist the lure of the enemy.

The Ears: Who and What My Child Listens To

> You have declared this day that the LORD is your God and that you will walk in obedience to him, that you will keep his decrees, commands and laws—that you will listen to him. (Deuteronomy 26:17)

I pray my child will declare this day that the Lord is their God and walk in obedience to You. I pray they will listen to Your voice and the voices of others that are consistent with Your teaching and Your Word. I also pray they will reject the voices that are inconsistent with Your truth.

The Mouth: Words My Child Speaks

> Don't use foul or abusive language. Let everything you say be good and helpful, so that your words will be an encouragement to those who hear them. (Ephesians 4:29 NLT)

I pray my child will not let any foul or abusive talk come out of their mouth but only words that are good and helpful to encourage those who hear them. I pray no coarse language, unclean jokes, or indecent innuendo will escape the door of my child's lips but only speech that is good, clean, and beneficial to build others up.

The Neck: Decisions That Turn My Child's Head

> I pray that your love will overflow more and more, and that you will keep on growing in knowledge and understanding. For I want you to understand what really matters, so that you may live pure and blameless lives until the day of Christ's return. (Philippians 1:9–10 NLT)

I pray my child's love for You will overflow and that they will keep on growing in knowledge and understanding. I pray they will understand what really matters so that they may live pure and blameless lives until the day of Christ's return. I pray my child will make good decisions based on godly discernment.

The Shoulders: Burdens and Worries

> The LORD himself goes before you and will be with you;
> he will never leave you nor forsake you. Do not be afraid;
> do not be discouraged. (Deuteronomy 31:8)

Thank You, Lord, for going before my child and always being with them. Help them remember that You will never leave nor forsake those who follow You, no matter what. Give my child the kind of solid faith that is not afraid of what the future holds or discouraged when circumstances become challenges. Help them trust in Your sovereign plan.

The Heart: Who and What My Child Loves

> Never let loyalty and kindness leave you! Tie them
> around your neck as a reminder. Write them deep within
> your heart. Then you will find favor with both God and
> people, and you will earn a good reputation. (Proverbs
> 3:3–4 NLT)

Lord, I pray my child will always be loyal and kind. I pray they will tie those qualities around their neck with the invisible cord of conviction and write those traits on their hearts with the indelible ink of devotion so that they will find favor with both God and people, earning a good reputation and a good name.

The Back: Physical and Spiritual Protection

> "Don't be afraid," the prophet answered. "Those who are with us are more than those who are with them." (2 Kings 6:16)

I pray warring angels will surround my child today. Thank You that Your power surrounding them is much greater than anyone or anything that might come against them. Even though my child most likely won't see Your mighty hosts with physical eyes, help them know they are there in the spiritual realm.

The Arms: Health and Strength

> LORD, be merciful to us, for we have waited for you. Be our strong arm each day and our salvation in times of trouble. (Isaiah 33:2 NLT)

I pray You will be my child's strong arm each day and their salvation in times of trouble. As they grow and mature, empower them to face any situation with courage and confidence. Protect them from peers who could persuade them to make ungodly decisions. Give my child the strength to resist following the wrong crowd.

The Hands: Gifts and Talents

> In everything he did he had great success, because the LORD was with him. (1 Samuel 18:14)

I pray my child will have great success in every pursuit that fits within Your plan. Help them know that accomplishments and achievements are a result of Your favor and presence in their lives.

The Ring Finger: Future Spouse

> Train up a child in the way he should go; even when he is
> old he will not depart from it. (Proverbs 22:6 ESV)

I pray You will give the parents of my child's future spouse wisdom on how to raise this individual. Help them recognize signature strengths so they can develop them, as well as potential weaknesses so they can fortify them. I pray they will know the best way to train up this special child in the way they should go so that they will never depart from it.

The Side: Influential Relationships

> The righteous choose their friends carefully, but the way
> of the wicked leads them astray. (Proverbs 12:26)

I pray my child will choose friends carefully. Keep them away from the wrong crowd, and point them to the right crowd.

Sexuality: Sexual Purity and Identity

> Promise me, O women of Jerusalem, not to awaken love
> until the time is right. (Song of Songs 8:4 NLT)

I pray my child will not awaken love until the time is right—that they will remain sexually pure until marriage.

> Scripture shows us that
> sex is not an evil that
> marriage permits but a gift
> that marriage protects.

The Legs: Stand for Godly Principles

> Choose for yourselves this day whom you will serve....
> But as for me and my household, we will serve the LORD.
> (Joshua 24:15b)

No matter what anyone else around my child is doing or saying, give them the determination to stand firm in the faith—never wavering in conviction.

The Knees: Relationship with God

> If you declare with your mouth, "Jesus is Lord," and
> believe in your heart that God raised him from the dead,
> you will be saved. (Romans 10:9)

I pray my child will declare, "Jesus is Lord," and believe that You raised Him from the dead so that they will be saved. I pray my child will accept

Jesus as Lord and Savior at an early age and continue to mature in faith as the years go by.

The Feet: The Path My Child Takes

> Trust in the LORD with all your heart and lean not on your own understanding; in all your ways submit to him, and he will make your paths straight. (Proverbs 3:5–6)

Lastly, I pray my child will trust in You with all their heart and lean not on their own understanding. I pray they will submit to You in all things and that You will make their path straight. I pray my child won't try to figure out everything on their own but will seek You and listen for Your voice.

Day 4

The Mind: What My Child Thinks About

> Now the serpent was more crafty than any of the wild animals the LORD God had made. He said to the woman, "Did God really say, 'You must not eat from any tree in the garden'?" (Genesis 3:1)

Dear Lord, I know that the same enemy that fed lies to Adam and Eve in the garden of Eden will try to feed lies to my child's mind. As he always does, the enemy will try to cause my child to doubt Your truth and question Your boundaries. Your word tells us that the devil is crafty and knows what lies to speak to each person. I pray my child will be alert to recognize his lies, quick to reject his lies, and determined to replace his lies with truth.

The Eyes: What My Child Looks At

> I will refuse to look at anything vile and vulgar. (Psalm 101:3a NLT)

I pray my child will not look at anything vile, vulgar, obnoxious, or offensive. Shield them from harmful images that could enter the mind through the portal of the eyes. Give them the willpower to click the delete button on the computer and the strength to turn their eyes away from harmful images.

The Ears: Who and What My Child Listens To

> It is better to heed the rebuke of a wise person than to listen to the song of fools. (Ecclesiastes 7:5)

I pray my child will be careful about music choices. I pray the song of fools will not enter their mind through the portal of the ears. Help my child to be discerning—sensitive to and aware of any words in a song that are contrary to Christian living. If a song is playing that could affect my child's heart in a negative way, I pray they will turn it off and choose music with more positive lyrics.

The Mouth: Words My Child Speaks

> Get rid of all bitterness, rage, anger, harsh words, and slander, as well as all types of evil behavior. Instead, be kind to each other, tenderhearted, forgiving one another, just as God through Christ has forgiven you. (Ephesians 4:31–32 NLT)

I pray my child will not speak bitter, angry, harsh, or slanderous words but only words that are kind, compassionate, and forgiving. If someone hurts, offends, or angers my child, I pray they will not retaliate with sharp words but with grace-filled speech.

The Neck: Decisions That Turn My Child's Head

> Do not conform to the pattern of this world, but be transformed by the renewing of your mind. Then you will be able to test and approve what God's will is—his good, pleasing and perfect will. (Romans 12:2)

I pray my child will not conform to the pattern, behavior, or attitudes of this world—that they will not make decisions based on what the world thinks is right or wrong, good or bad, acceptable or unacceptable but will make decisions based on what Scripture says is right or wrong, good or bad, acceptable or unacceptable. I pray my child will be able to understand what Your will is—Your good, pleasing, and perfect will.

The Shoulders: Burdens and Worries

> Those who know your name trust in you, for you, LORD, have never forsaken those who seek you. (Psalm 9:10)

Thank You, Lord, that You never forsake or abandon those who seek You. I pray my child will seek You in all circumstances and that You will lift any burdens of worry or anxiety from their shoulders. Teach my child to rest in, lean on, and confidently trust in You.

The Heart: Who and What My Child Loves

> Where your treasure is, there your heart will be also. (Matthew 6:21 ESV)

I know that where my child's treasure is, that's where their heart will be also. I pray they will love what You love. Fill the safety deposit box of my child's heart with treasures that cannot be stolen, will not rust, and will not lose value over time. Remind them that the most valuable treasure of all, the pearl of great price, is found in a personal relationship with You.

The Back: Physical and Spiritual Protection

> He [Nebuchadnezzar] said, "Look! I see four men walking around in the fire, unbound and unharmed, and the fourth looks like a son of the gods." (Daniel 3:25)

Gracious God, just as you protected Shadrach, Meshach, and Abednego in Nebuchadnezzar's fiery furnace, protect my child from the fiery furnaces of this world. No matter how difficult the circumstances my child must face, guide each step along the path—delivering them unscathed and unscarred, without even a hint of smoke. May Jesus' protecting presence be evident to my child and to those watching their life.

The Arms: Health and Strength

> The LORD commissioned Joshua the son of Nun and said, "Be strong and courageous, for you shall bring the people of Israel into the land that I swore to give them. I will be with you." (Deuteronomy 31:23 ESV)

Empower my child to be strong and courageous to do everything You have called them to do. Fill my child with the power of the Holy Spirit to withstand the ungodly patterns and practices of the culture.

The Hands: Gifts and Talents

> May the favor of the Lord our God rest on us; establish
> the work of our hands for us—yes, establish the work of
> our hands. (Psalm 90:17)

May Your favor rest upon my child today, Lord God. Establish the work of their hands, and give them great success. Whether it's schoolwork, teamwork, or artwork, encourage them to strive to do their best.

If children listen to the wrong voices, they will make wrong choices.

The Ring Finger: Future Spouse

> My prayer is not that you take them out of the world but
> that you protect them from the evil one. (John 17:15)

Father, I pray You will protect my child's future spouse from the evil one in each area of this individual's life: spiritual, emotional, and physical.

The Side: Influential Relationships

> How good and and pleasant it is when God's people live
> together in unity! (Psalm 133:1)

I pray my child will enjoy living in unity with friends, family, and fellow
believers. Help them to be a peacemaker and not a pot stirrer.

Sexuality: Sexual Purity and Identity

> Do you not know that your bodies are temples of the Holy
> Spirit, who is in you, whom you have received from God?
> You are not your own; you were bought at a price. Therefore
> honor God with your bodies. (1 Corinthians 6:19–20)

I pray my child will always remember that they are a temple of the Holy
Spirit who was bought by the blood of Jesus. I pray my child will honor
You with their body in all they do.

The Legs: Stand for Godly Principles

> It is God who arms me with strength and keeps my way
> secure. He makes my feet like the feet of a deer; he causes
> me to stand on the heights. (2 Samuel 22:33–34)

Almighty God, I pray my child will develop a strong stand for truth.
Help them stand firm in faith, even when others teeter on the cliffs of
uncertainty. Give my child strength to stand upright on the heights
of moral character and wisdom to navigate the rocky terrain of this
wavering world.

The Knees: Relationship with God

> God so loved the world that he gave his one and only Son, that whoever believes in him shall not perish but have eternal life. (John 3:16)

Thank You, God, that You loved me and my child so much that You gave Your one and only Son to die for our sins and make it possible for us to live in eternity with You. I pray my child will bow the knee and believe in Jesus as Lord and Savior. I thank You in advance for that miraculous day.

The Feet: The Path My Child Takes

> Walk in obedience to all that the LORD your God has commanded you, so that you may live and prosper and prolong your days in the land that you will possess. (Deuteronomy 5:33)

Finally, I pray my child will walk in all the ways the Lord God has commanded so that they may live a long prosperous life. Hem my child in so that their feet will not veer to the right or the left. Keep each step firmly on the path You have marked out for them. I pray all this in Jesus' name, amen.

Day 5

The Mind: What My Child Thinks About

He [the devil] has always hated the truth, because there is no truth in him. When he lies, it is consistent with his character; for he is a liar and the father of lies. (John 8:44b NLT)

Dear Lord, I pray You will protect my child's mind from the evil one's influence. Because every spiritual battle is won or lost at the threshold of the mind, I pray my child will not answer the door when the enemy knocks. I pray they will not allow the enemy's lies to enter through the mind's door to influence their thinking. I pray You will help my child recognize the enemy's lies quickly, reject them completely, and replace his lies with Your truth.

The Eyes: What My Child Looks At

I made a covenant with my eyes not to look lustfully at a young woman. (Job 31:1)

Lord, I pray my child will not look at the opposite sex with lustful eyes and impure thoughts. Even though our world teems with sexual imagery, I pray they will avert their gaze when tempted to look.

The Ears: Who and What My Child Listens To

> He wakens me morning by morning, wakens my ear to
> listen like one being instructed. (Isaiah 50:4b)

I pray You will waken my child morning by morning, waken their ears like one being taught. I pray they will grow into a spiritually mature person who recognizes Your articulate presence all day long.

The Mouth: Words My Child Speaks

> Do everything without grumbling or arguing. (Philip-
> pians 2:14)

I pray my child will do everything that must be done today without grumbling, arguing, or complaining but instead do it cheerfully, willingly, and agreeably.

The Neck: Decisions That Turn My Child's Head

> The LORD said to Samuel, "Do not consider his appear-
> ance or his height, for I have rejected him. The LORD
> does not look at the things people look at. People look
> at the outward appearance, but the LORD looks at the
> heart." (1 Samuel 16:7)

As my child makes choices that will turn their head one way or the other, I pray they will look beyond the outward appearance of a situation to the inner motivation of the action.

The Shoulders: Burdens and Worries

> The LORD is my shepherd; I have all that I need. (Psalm
> 23:1 NLT)

Lord, thank You for being the Great Shepherd who leads, protects, and cares for my child. Help them not to worry about the future or about fitting in with others, because You are everything they need.

The Heart: Who and What My Child Loves

> The peace of God, which transcends all understanding,
> will guard your hearts and your minds in Christ Jesus.
> (Philippians 4:7)

Thank You, God, for the gift of Your peace, which is beyond our ability to understand or explain. May that peace guard and protect my child's heart from the world, the flesh, and the devil. I ask You to keep their heart under the surveillance of Your all-seeing eyes and behind the fortress of Your protective care.

The Back: Physical and Spiritual Protection

> Have you not put a hedge around him and his household
> and everything he has? (Job 1:10a)

Almighty Lord, I pray You will place a hedge of protection around my child today. Preserve my child's going out and coming in. Keep all that is good in and all that is evil out.

The Arms: Health and Strength

> Be strong and courageous. Do not be afraid or terrified
> because of them, for the LORD your God goes with you; he
> will never leave you nor forsake you. (Deuteronomy 31:6)

I pray my child will be strong and courageous today—that they will not be afraid of or terrified by outside forces. Remind them that You, the ultimate force, are with us wherever we may go.

The Hands: Gifts and Talents

> A little sleep, a little slumber, a little folding of the hands
> to rest, and poverty will come upon you like a robber, and
> want like an armed man. (Proverbs 6:10–11 ESV)

I pray my child will not be lazy but will use their hands to be productive and prosperous.

The Ring Finger: Future Spouse

> The righteous choose their friends carefully, but the way
> of the wicked leads them astray. (Proverbs 12:26)

Protect my child's future spouse from the wrong kind of friends, and propel them to the right kind of friends. Lead my child's future spouse to friends who have a heart for You and a desire to do good and to be good.

The Side: Influential Relationships

> A generous person will prosper; whoever refreshes others
> will be refreshed. (Proverbs 11:25)

Gracious God, I pray my child will be a generous person who uses resources, time, words, and actions to refresh others. As they pour love and kindness into others, I pray You will pour back into them.

Sexuality: Sexual Purity and Identity

> Flee from sexual immorality. All other sins a person commits are outside the body, but whoever sins sexually, sins against their own body. (1 Corinthians 6:18)

I pray my child will flee sexual immorality and remain pure until marriage. When temptation to engage in sexually promiscuous behavior arises, I pray my child will run in the opposite direction.

The Legs: Stand for Godly Principles

> Elijah went before the people and said, "How long will you waver between two opinions? If the LORD is God, follow him; but if Baal is God, follow him." (1 Kings 18:21)

I pray my child will never waver between faithfulness and faithlessness but stand firm in the decision to follow You.

The Knees: Relationship with God

> Like newborn babies, crave pure spiritual milk, so that by it you may grow up in your salvation, now that you have tasted that the Lord is good. (1 Peter 2:2–3)

Now that my child has tasted what it means to know You by what they have experienced in our home, I pray they will crave the pure spiritual milk of Your Word, ultimately growing into a spiritually strong follower of Christ with an ever-maturing faith.

The Feet: The Path My Child Takes

> I have no greater joy than to hear that my children are walking in the truth. (3 John 1:4 ESV)

Finally, I have no greater joy than to hear that my child is walking in the truth. I pray they will walk on the path of truth, in the light of truth, and with the surefootedness of truth all the days of their life. I pray all this in Jesus' name, amen.

Day 6

The Mind: What My Child Thinks About

Those who live according to the flesh have their minds set on what the flesh desires; but those who live in accordance with the Spirit have their minds set on what the Spirit desires. (Romans 8:5)

Dear Lord, I pray my child's mind will be set on what the Spirit desires today: love, joy, peace, patience, kindness, goodness, faithfulness, gentleness, and self-control. When the desires of the flesh try to weasel their way in, I pray You will help my child recognize the enemy's tactics quickly and reject the thoughts completely.

The Eyes: What My Child Looks At

Ears that hear and eyes that see—the LORD has made them both. (Proverbs 20:12)

Creator God, thank You for giving my child ears that hear and eyes that see. I pray they will see You in creation, in other people, in Your Word, and in everyday circumstances. Give them clear vision throughout life to discern good and evil, light and darkness, right and wrong.

The Ears: Who and What My Child Listens To

> Faith comes from hearing, and hearing through the word
> of Christ. (Romans 10:17 ESV)

I pray my child will listen to music and messages that strengthen their faith
and turn away from music and messages that would weaken their faith.

The Mouth: Words My Child Speaks

> Our mouths were filled with laughter, our tongues with
> songs of joy. Then it was said among the nations, "The
> LORD has done great things for them." (Psalm 126:2)

I pray my child's mouth will be filled with laughter and their tongue
with songs of joy so that others will say, "The Lord has done great
things for them!"

The Neck: Decisions That Turn My Child's Head

> When he had finished speaking, he said to Simon, "Put out
> into deep water, and let down the nets for a catch." Simon
> answered, "Master, we've worked hard all night and haven't
> caught anything. But because you say so, I will let down
> the nets." When they had done so, they caught such a large
> number of fish that their nets began to break. (Luke 5:4–6)

Lord, as my child is making decisions today, I pray they will be like
Simon, who, even though he didn't understand why he needed to do
what Jesus asked him to do, obeyed anyway. Even if what You're telling
my child to do doesn't seem to make sense, I pray they will respond, "But

because you say so, I will." Bless the fruit of my child's obedience beyond human comprehension or man's explanation.

The Shoulders: Burdens and Worries

> I sought the LORD, and he answered me and delivered me from all my fears. (Psalm 34:4 ESV)

When my child begins to feel the weight of the world pressing down on those shoulders, I pray they will stop and ask You to deliver them from fear and worry. Whether it's schoolwork or school violence, friendship tension or family dynamics, body image or outward appearance, help my child remember that they are completely accepted and uniquely fashioned for divine purposes.

The Heart: Who and What My Child Loves

> Do not love this world nor the things it offers you, for when you love the world, you do not have the love of the Father in you. For the world offers only a craving for physical pleasure, a craving for everything we see, and pride in our achievements and possessions. These are not from the Father, but are from this world. And this world is fading away, along with everything that people crave. But anyone who does what pleases God will live forever. (1 John 2:15–17 NLT)

I pray my child will not love the world or the things of this world more than You. Help them understand that the world only offers cravings for physical pleasure, cravings for everything we see, and pride in our achievements and possessions. You have so much more for us than that.

Let my child see that this world and everything in it is passing away but life with You lasts forever.

The Back: Physical and Spiritual Protection

> You, O LORD, are a shield about me, my glory, and the
> lifter of my head. (Psalm 3:3 ESV)

Almighty God, I pray You will be a shield around my child today, covering them from head to toe and from front to back. Deliver my child from evil, and protect them from harm. I pray You will put Your finger under their chin and lift their gaze heavenward.

The Arms: Health and Strength

> Have I not commanded you? Be strong and courageous.
> Do not be afraid; do not be discouraged, for the LORD
> your God will be with you wherever you go. (Joshua 1:9)

Fill my child with the power of the Holy Spirit so that they will be strong and courageous today. Protect my child from discouragement and despair with the comforting truth that You are with those who follow You wherever we may go.

The Hands: Gifts and Talents

> Work hard and become a leader; be lazy and become a
> slave. (Proverbs 12:24 NLT)

I pray my child will work hard and become a leader—never being lazy or dependent on others.

The Ring Finger: Future Spouse

> Love the Lord your God with all your heart and with
> all your soul and with all your mind and with all your
> strength.... Love your neighbor as yourself. (Mark
> 12:30–31)

Lord, I pray my child's future spouse will grow up to deeply love You with all their heart, soul, mind, and strength—and that my child's future spouse will strive to be a person after Your own heart. I also pray they will be a person who loves others—someone who is kind, caring, and compassionate.

> What children think
> about will ultimately
> determine what
> they are about.

The Side: Influential Relationships

> Do not be misled: "Bad company corrupts good charac-
> ter." (1 Corinthians 15:33)

I pray my child will not be misled by thinking they can hang around with immoral people and walk away unaffected. Help them to always remember that bad company corrupts good character. Give my child the desire to make close friends with people who exhibit qualities of integrity, honesty, and morality.

Sexuality: Sexual Purity and Identity

> In those days Israel had no king; all the people did whatever seemed right in their own eyes. (Judges 17:6 NLT)

Father, it seems our culture is a reflection of the Israelites in the days of the judges—living like there is no reigning God and no ruling truth—doing what is right in their own eyes. The world is attempting to erase sexual boundaries and celebrates immoral depravity. I pray my child will not have an attitude of "If it feels good do it" but a conviction of "If God says don't do it, it is for my own good."

The Legs: Stand for Godly Principles

> You will not have to fight this battle. Take up your positions; stand firm and see the deliverance the LORD will give you, Judah and Jerusalem. Do not be afraid; do not be discouraged. Go out to face them tomorrow, and the LORD will be with you. (2 Chronicles 20:17)

Almighty God, reassure my child that You fight our battles for us. Show them how to take up the position as a child of God. Teach my child how to stand firm in the knowledge of who they are in Christ. Help them to not be afraid or discouraged but to feel secure and sure—empowered to go out and face the day with confidence. Help my child know that they are a chosen, holy child of God who is equipped by the Father, enveloped by the Son, and empowered by the Holy Spirit.

The Knees: Relationship with God

> For this reason, since the day we heard about you, we have not stopped praying for you. We continually ask God to fill you with the knowledge of his will through all the wisdom and understanding that the Spirit gives, so that you may live a life worthy of the Lord and please him in every way: bearing fruit in every good work, growing in the knowledge of God. (Colossians 1:9–10)

Father, I will never stop praying for my child—continually asking You to fill them with the knowledge of Your will through all wisdom and understanding that the Spirit gives so that my child may live a life worthy of You and pleasing You in every way: bearing fruit in every good work, growing in the knowledge of God.

The Feet: The Path My Child Takes

> Whoever walks in integrity walks securely, but he who makes his ways crooked will be found out. (Proverbs 10:9 ESV)

Lastly, I pray You will keep my child from walking a path of dishonesty that leads to scrutiny and self-destruction and that You will help them stay on a path of integrity that leads to safety and security. I pray all this in Jesus' name, amen.

Day 7

The Mind: What My Child Thinks About

> The thief comes only to steal and kill and destroy; I have
> come that they may have life, and have it to the full.
> (John 10:10)

Heavenly Father, I pray You will protect my child's mind against the lies of the enemy, who seeks to steal, kill, and destroy. I pray You will place a wall of protection around my child's thought life—that You will keep out thoughts that lead to discouragement, discontentment, and destruction and usher in thoughts that lead to the abundant life Jesus came to give.

The Eyes: What My Child Looks At

> My ears had heard of you but now my eyes have seen you.
> (Job 42:5)

Even though my child has heard about You in our home, I pray they will see You actively working in everyday life.

The Ears: Who and What My Child Listens To

Listen to me, you who pursue righteousness, you who seek
the LORD: look to the rock from which you were hewn, and
to the quarry from which you were dug. (Isaiah 51:1 ESV)

I pray my child will listen to You and pursue righteousness. May they
seek You and pursue a deep relationship with You. I pray they will look
to Jesus, the Rock of our salvation, and remember Him always.

The Mouth: Words My Child Speaks

Set a guard over my mouth, LORD; keep watch over the
door of my lips. (Psalm 141:3)

I pray You will set a guard over my child's mouth, Lord. Keep watch
over the door of their lips. I pray You will not let any unwise or ungodly
words escape the door of my child's mouth, no matter how badly they
want to get out.

The Neck: Decisions That Turn My Child's Head

No temptation has overtaken you except what is common
to mankind. And God is faithful; he will not let you be
tempted beyond what you can bear. But when you are
tempted, he will also provide a way out so that you can
endure it. (1 Corinthians 10:13)

When my child is tempted to make a decision that is contrary to Christian character, I pray they will turn and go in the opposite direction. Help my child realize that these temptations are nothing new and no different from what anyone else experiences. Thank You, God, that You will never allow my child to be tempted beyond what they are able to resist. Thank You for always providing a way of escape. I pray my child will see it and have the moral fortitude to take it.

The Shoulders: Burdens and Worries

> Why, my soul, are you downcast? Why so disturbed within me? Put your hope in God, for I will yet praise him, my Savior and my God. (Psalm 42:5)

When my child feels the pressure of this world bearing down, remind them that You are the Burden-Bearer! When my child feels all tied up in knots, loosen the cords of worry with the fingers of praise and help them remember all the good things about life.

The Heart: Who and What My Child Loves

> He has shown you, O mortal, what is good. And what does the LORD require of you? To act justly and to love mercy and to walk humbly with your God. (Micah 6:8)

I pray my child will love mercy and have compassion on those in need, that they will not become hardhearted or judgmental of those who are less fortunate.

The Back: Physical and Spiritual Protection

> Let all who take refuge in you be glad; let them ever sing
> for joy. Spread your protection over them, that those who
> love your name may rejoice in you. (Psalm 5:11)

All-powerful Father, I pray You will spread Your protective canopy over
my child today. Keep them from harm in both the physical and spiritual
realms.

The Arms: Health and Strength

> Look to the LORD and his strength; seek his face always.
> (1 Chronicles 16:11)

I pray my child will look to You and Your strength, that they will seek
You always. Whether it is strength to follow You or strength to not fol-
low the crowd, I pray my child will not rely on human willpower but on
Your mighty power.

The Hands: Gifts and Talents

> May the favor of the Lord our God rest on us; establish
> the work of our hands for us—yes, establish the work of
> our hands. (Psalm 90:17)

I pray Your favor will rest upon my child and that You will establish the
work of their hands, making their efforts successful.

The Ring Finger: Future Spouse

> Trust in the LORD with all your heart and lean not on your own understanding; in all your ways submit to him, and he will make your paths straight. (Proverbs 3:5–6)

I pray my child's future spouse will not lean on their own understanding, trying to figure out everything through human reason, but will trust in You and submit to You, knowing You will make the path straight and clear.

The Side: Influential Relationships

> As iron sharpens iron, so one person sharpens another. (Proverbs 27:17)

I pray You will bless my child with friends who will sharpen "as iron sharpens iron"—those who will challenge, inspire, and hold them accountable. Give my child the wisdom and grace to do the same for their friends.

Sexuality: Sexual Purity and Identity

> Watch and pray so that you will not fall into temptation. The spirit is willing, but the flesh is weak. (Mark 14:38)

Lord, in this oversexualized culture we live in, it is so hard not to fall into sexual temptation. I pray my child will have the courage to turn away from the sexual promiscuity and moral ambiguity that is celebrated on social media, on television, and across the internet. Help them turn away from alluring images and invitations and turn toward what is acceptable and pure.

The Legs: Stand for Godly Principles

> I have set the LORD always before me; because he is at my
> right hand, I shall not be shaken. (Psalm 16:8 ESV)

I pray my child will keep You at the center of life. Help them stand firm in the truth and not be shaken by the shifting values and shady morality of our culture. Don't let them falter in faith or cower in fear. I pray You will help my child face every situation with the full confidence that You are at our right hand, sustaining and supporting us.

The Knees: Relationship with God

> Just as you received Christ Jesus as Lord, continue to live
> your lives in him, rooted and built up in him, strength-
> ened in the faith as you were taught, and overflowing
> with thankfulness. (Colossians 2:6–7)

I pray my child will receive Christ Jesus as Lord at an early age and then continue to live life rooted, built up, and strengthened in the faith as they mature. May my child overflow with thankfulness and gratitude for all You have done and continue to do.

The Feet: The Path My Child Takes

> You make known to me the path of life; you will fill me
> with joy in your presence, with eternal pleasures at your
> right hand. (Psalm 16:11)

Finally, I pray my child will walk the path of life You have marked out for them. Fill my child with joy, peace, and the ability to walk in constant communion and unbroken union with You. Allow my child to experience eternal pleasures of joy in Your presence as they take hold of Your right hand. I pray all this in Jesus' name, amen.

Day 8

The Mind: What My Child Thinks About

Don't copy the behavior and customs of this world, but let God transform you into a new person by changing the way you think. Then you will learn to know God's will for you, which is good and pleasing and perfect. (Romans 12:2 NLT)

I pray my child will not simply copy the behavior and customs of this world but will let You transform their mind to think biblically. I pray You will weed out any thoughts that do not line up with Your Word and plant new thoughts that will help them grow into the spiritually mature person You have created them to be. Then they will know Your good and perfect will.

The Eyes: What My Child Looks At

The precepts of the LORD are right, giving joy to the heart. The commands of the LORD are radiant, giving light to the eyes. (Psalm 19:8)

I pray the Holy Spirit will give light to my child's eyes so that they will be able to discern the difference between right and wrong, life and death, moral and immoral, and God's truth versus the world's lies.

The Ears: Who and What My Child Listens To

> While you were doing all these things, declares the LORD,
> I spoke to you again and again, but you did not listen; I
> called you, but you did not answer. (Jeremiah 7:13)

I pray my child will not be like the Israelites, who did not listen to You, but instead recognize Your voice quickly and respond immediately.

The Mouth: Words My Child Speaks

> Those who guard their lips preserve their lives, but those
> who speak rashly will come to ruin. (Proverbs 13:3)

I pray my child will guard their lips—that they will be careful to speak reasonably and reflectively and not recklessly or rashly.

The Neck: Decisions That Turn My Child's Head

> Do not be stiff-necked, as your ancestors were; submit to
> the LORD. (2 Chronicles 30:8a)

I pray my child will not be stiff-necked—bullheaded and stubborn, doing what they want to do when they want to do it. Instead, I pray my child will choose to be submissive to You and do what You want them to do when You want it done.

The Shoulders: Burdens and Worries

> Praise be to the Lord, to God our Savior, who daily bears
> our burdens. (Psalm 68:19)

Lord, the burdens of growing up can be so hard. Thank You for being our Burden-Bearer. Thank You for never getting tired of our burdens or weary under them. I pray my child will release their burdens and place them on Your able shoulders—today and every day.

The Heart: Who and What My Child Loves

> Delight yourself in the LORD, and he will give you the
> desires of your heart. (Psalm 37:4 ESV)

I pray my child will delight in a relationship with You—that they will enjoy being in Your presence and reading Your Word. I pray that as my child grows closer to You, their desires will line up with Your desires.

The Back: Physical and Spiritual Protection

> [Jesus prayed,] Holy Father, protect them by the power of
> your name, the name you gave me, so that they may be
> one as we are one. (John 17:11b)

Just as Jesus asked You to protect His friends by the power of Your name, I ask You to protect my child by the power of Jesus' name.

The Arms: Health and Strength

> David also said to Solomon his son, "Be strong and
> courageous, and do the work. Do not be afraid or

discouraged, for the LORD God, my God, is with you."
(1 Chronicles 28:20a)

Just as David instructed his child to be strong and courageous, I pray that same thing for mine. Enable my child to be strong and courageous to do the work You have called them to do. I pray against the spirit of discouragement and for power of determination.

The Hands: Gifts and Talents

She opens her hand to the poor and reaches out her hands to the needy. (Proverbs 31:20 ESV)

I pray my child will open their hands to the poor and reach out to the needy. May they use the gifts and talents You have given to help others.

The Ring Finger: Future Spouse

You have always put a wall of protection around him and his home and his property. (Job 1:10a NLT)

God, I pray You will place a wall of protection around my child's future spouse. Please put up a barrier to keep out anyone or anything that would cause harm spiritually, physically, or emotionally.

The Side: Influential Relationships

A friend loves at all times. (Proverbs 17:17a ESV)

Lord, teach my child what it means to be a friend who loves at all times, especially when someone is hard to love. Also, I pray You will bless them with a friend who will do likewise: choosing to extend love when my child is the one who is difficult to love.

Sexuality: Sexual Purity and Identity

> The body ... is not meant for sexual immorality but for the Lord, and the Lord for the body. (1 Corinthians 6:13b)

Thank You for the gift of sexual intimacy in marriage. I pray my child will protect this gift until it can be given freely and without shame, guilt, or regret on their wedding night.

The Legs: Stand for Godly Principles

> Some trust in chariots and some in horses, but we trust in the name of the LORD our God. They are brought to their knees and fall, but we rise up and stand firm. (Psalm 20:7–8)

Lord God, I pray my child will not put their trust in people, peers, popularity, or possessions but in You. When those around them buckle under the world's pressure—conforming to ungodly principles and unholy practices—give my child the courage to rise up and stand firm on what is right.

The Knees: Relationship with God

> For this very reason, make every effort to add to your faith goodness; and to goodness, knowledge; and to knowledge, self-control; and to self-control, perseverance; and to perseverance, godliness; and to godliness, mutual affection; and to mutual affection, love. (2 Peter 1:5–7)

I pray my child will not simply stop at accepting Jesus as Savior but continue to grow spiritually strong by making every effort to grow in faith, adding goodness, knowledge, self-control, perseverance, godliness, mutual affection, and love.

The Feet: The Path My Child Takes

He makes my feet like the feet of a deer, he enables me to tread on the heights. (Habakkuk 3:19b)

Finally, Lord, I pray You will make my child's feet like the feet of a deer and enable them to stand surefooted on the rocky heights. Keep my child secure and confident on the crossroads of conflict and the rough terrain of trials. I pray all this in Jesus' name, amen.

Day 9

The Mind: What My Child Thinks About

Though we live in the world, we do not wage war as the world does. The weapons we fight with are not the weapons of the world. On the contrary, they have divine power to demolish strongholds. We demolish arguments and every pretension that sets itself up against the knowledge of God, and we take captive every thought to make it obedient to Christ. (2 Corinthians 10:3–5)

Dear Lord, the world is full of ideas and beliefs that run contrary to the truth. As my child maneuvers through a maze of misguided ideas of right and wrong, I pray You will help them take captive every thought that could lead in the wrong direction. I pray my child will not buy into what the culture is selling but use every spiritual weapon You have given to fight against worldly lies. Help them take every thought captive to make it obedient to Christ.

The Eyes: What My Child Looks At

I remain confident of this: I will see the goodness of the LORD in the land of the living. (Psalm 27:13)

I pray my child will see the goodness of the Lord throughout the day. I pray they will not be so distracted by all that is going on that they miss all that You are doing.

The Ears: Who and What My Child Listens To

> They did not listen or pay attention; instead, they followed the stubborn inclinations of their evil hearts. They went backward and not forward. (Jeremiah 7:24)

I pray my child will listen and pay attention to You and Your Word. I pray they will not follow the stubborn inclination of the heart that says, "I want what I want when I want it." I pray my child will listen to Your instruction, moving forward and not backward, being obedient and not defiant.

The Mouth: Words My Child Speaks

> Even fools are thought wise if they keep silent, and discerning if they hold their tongues. (Proverbs 17:28)

I pray my child will keep silent when it is best to do so. Give them discernment to know when to hold their tongue and keep their thoughts and opinions to themselves.

The Neck: Decisions That Turn My Child's Head

> Give me an understanding heart so that I can govern your people well and know the difference between right and wrong. (1 Kings 3:9a NLT)

Lord, just as King Solomon prayed for discernment and understanding to govern his people, I pray my child will have discernment and understanding to distinguish between right and wrong, good and evil, now or later. May their decisions be based on moral character rather than man's opinions.

The Shoulders: Burdens and Worries

> I have cared for you since you were born. Yes, I carried you before you were born. I will be your God throughout your lifetime—until your hair is white with age. I made you, and I will care for you. I will carry you along and save you. (Isaiah 46:3b–4 NLT)

God, thank You for caring for my child even before they were born. I am so thankful that You will be my child's God through their lifetime—until their hair is white with age. I pray my child will always remember that You are our Creator and that You never stop caring for us. Thank You for promising to carry my child throughout life and to save them for eternity.

The Heart: Who and What My Child Loves

> He heals the brokenhearted and binds up their wounds. (Psalm 147:3 ESV)

Father, I know at some point my child will experience a broken heart. When that happens, I pray You will bring healing and bind up any emotional wounds.

If they do not
stand on the truth,
the world becomes
a confusing place.
The undertow of
uncertainty can
pull them out to
sea with a riptide
of questions and
the shifting tides
of change.

The Back: Physical and Spiritual Protection

The LORD is my light and my salvation—whom shall I fear? The LORD is the stronghold of my life—of whom shall I be afraid? (Psalm 27:1)

I pray my child will know that You are our light and our salvation; therefore, they don't need to fear anything that comes their way. Thank You for being our strong tower, deliverer, and shield—a mighty fortress of protection.

The Arms: Health and Strength

In your hand are power and might, and in your hand it is to make great and to give strength to all. (1 Chronicles 29:12b ESV)

Lord, please give my child physical, emotional, and spiritual strength today. Make them a conduit through which Your mighty power flows.

The Hands: Gifts and Talents

Never be lazy, but work hard and serve the Lord enthusiastically. (Romans 12:11 NLT)

I pray my child will not be lazy or lackadaisical but will work energetically and enthusiastically.

The Ring Finger: Future Spouse

He will cover you with his feathers. He will shelter you with his wings. His faithful promises are your armor and protection. (Psalm 91:4 NLT)

Lord, I pray You will cover my child's future spouse with Your feathers and shelter them with Your wings. Just as a baby chick runs to the shelter of its mother's wings, I pray my child's future spouse will run to the shelter of Your protective care.

The Side: Influential Relationships

> [Love] keeps no record of wrongs. (1 Corinthians 13:5b)

I pray my child will not keep a record of wrongs in their relationships but will forgive quickly and completely, just as You have forgiven them.

Sexuality: Sexual Purity and Identity

> Don't let us yield to temptation, but rescue us from the evil one. (Matthew 6:13 NLT)

I pray my child will not yield to sexual temptation but that You will rescue them from the evil one who seeks to devalue and depreciate the gift of physical intimacy.

The Legs: Stand for Godly Principles

> Now I stand on solid ground, and I will publicly praise the LORD. (Psalm 26:12 NLT)

I pray my child will stand firm on the level ground of Your truth and not wobble on the shifting sand of the world's relative conformity and moral ambiguity that changes what is right and wrong, true and false, fact and fiction on any given day.

The Knees: Relationship with God

> Oh come, let us worship and bow down; let us kneel
> before the LORD, our Maker! For he is our God, and we
> are the people of his pasture, and the sheep of his hand.
> (Psalm 95:6–7a ESV)

Father God, I pray my child will have a humble spirit that willingly bows down and worships You as Lord, Maker, and Master. Thank You for being my child's Shepherd, keeping them under Your care.

The Feet: The Path My Child Takes

> Even though I walk through the valley of the shadow of
> death, I fear no evil, for You are with me; Your rod and
> Your staff, they comfort me. (Psalm 23:4 NASB)

Finally, even if my child must one day walk through a dark valley, a difficult circumstance, or a life-threatening situation, I pray they will not be afraid. Blanket my child with peace—the comfort of knowing that You are right there, step by step, along the way. Prod my child forward with Your rod when they lag behind, and pull them back with Your staff when they run ahead. I pray all this in Jesus' name, amen.

Day 10

The Mind: What My Child Thinks About

> Be careful how you think; your life is shaped by your thoughts. (Proverbs 4:23 GNT)

I pray my child will be careful about what they think, realizing that our lives are shaped by our thoughts. When my child notices an ungodly, unkind, or unclean thought creeping in, I pray they will have the wisdom and the will to refuse its entrance.

The Eyes: What My Child Looks At

> God opened her [Hagar's] eyes and she saw a well of water. (Genesis 21:19a)

Just as You opened Hagar's eyes to see the well of water that had been there all along, I pray You will open my child's eyes to see all the many ways You are with them throughout the day.

The Ears: Who and What My Child Listens To

> You warned them in order to turn them back to your law, but they became arrogant and disobeyed your

commands. They sinned against your ordinances, of which you said, "The person who obeys them will live by them." Stubbornly they turned their backs on you, became stiff-necked and refused to listen. (Nehemiah 9:29)

I pray my child will not be arrogant and refuse to listen to Your commands but will be compliant to obey Your ordinances. I pray they will experience the blessings of living life in tandem with Your Word.

The Mouth: Words My Child Speaks

A gentle answer turns away wrath, but a harsh word stirs up anger. (Proverbs 15:1)

No matter what someone says to irritate or anger my child today, I pray they will not respond to harsh words with hurtful words that add fuel to the fire but with kind words that quench the flames.

The Neck: Decisions That Turn My Child's Head

He gives wisdom to the wise and knowledge to the discerning. (Daniel 2:21b)

Lord, just as You gave Daniel wisdom to make the best decisions, even when it meant contradicting the culture in which he lived, I ask You to give my child wisdom to make the best decisions despite the culture in which we live. Bless my child with supernatural knowledge and spot-on discernment for every choice they make today.

The Shoulders: Burdens and Worries

> "I know the plans I have for you," declares the LORD,
> "plans to prosper you and not to harm you, plans to give
> you hope and a future." (Jeremiah 29:11)

Father, I stand on the promise that You have a perfect plan for my child, plans to prosper and not to harm, plans to give a future and a hope. Help my child to not worry about present circumstances or future happenstances but rest in the knowledge that You always have their best interest in mind.

The Heart: Who and What My Child Loves

> I pray that out of his glorious riches he may strengthen
> you with power through his Spirit in your inner being,
> so that Christ may dwell in your hearts through faith.
> (Ephesians 3:16–17a)

Father, I pray You will strengthen and empower my child in their inner being with the power of the Holy Spirit. I pray Jesus will feel at home in their heart and make it a permanent dwelling place.

The Back: Physical and Spiritual Protection

> We are not unaware of his [Satan's] schemes. (2 Corinthians 2:11b)

Lord, I am not unaware of the devil's schemes. I know he wants to kill, steal, and destroy and would like nothing better than to squirm his way into my child's life. I pray against the schemes of the devil in the name of Jesus.

The Arms: Health and Strength

> As for you, be strong and do not give up, for your work
> will be rewarded. (2 Chronicles 15:7)

Lord, I pray You will strengthen my child so that they will not give up when life gets tough but, instead, step up to do all You've called them to do. I ask that You equip, energize, and encourage my child with the power of the Holy Spirit, rewarding them for a job well done.

The Hands: Gifts and Talents

> Do not neglect your gift, which was given you through
> prophecy when the body of elders laid their hands on you.
> (1 Timothy 4:14)

I pray my child will not neglect the spiritual, intellectual, physical, or creative gifts You have given them but develop those gifts to glorify You.

The Ring Finger: Future Spouse

> You hem me in behind and before, and you lay your hand
> upon me. (Psalm 139:5)

I pray You will hem my child's future spouse in behind and before and lay Your hand upon them. Keep this person whom we've yet to meet safe and secure.

The Side: Influential Relationships

> Make up your mind not to put any stumbling block or
> obstacle in the way of a brother or sister. (Romans 14:13b)

Lord, I pray my child will never put a stumbling block or obstacle in a friend's way. Give them the determination to not speak any words or exhibit any behavior that would hinder or handicap a friend's spiritual growth or moral decisions. Likewise, I pray none of my child's friends will put a stumbling block in their path.

Sexuality: Sexual Purity and Identity

> A person without self-control is like a city with broken-
> down walls. (Proverbs 25:28 NLT)

I pray my child will not be like an ancient city whose walls are broken down—a city that is unprotected and vulnerable to attacks. Rather, I pray my child will be like a fortified city with sturdy walls of protection to guard them from attacks of temptation and moral weakness. Give my child self-control and self-restraint to ward off sexual temptation.

The Legs: Stand for Godly Principles

> He lifted me out of the slimy pit, out of the mud and
> mire; he set my feet on a rock and gave me a firm place to
> stand. (Psalm 40:2)

During those moments when my child may feel as if the ground is sinking into a pit of despair, discouragement, or depression, I pray You will lift them out of those slimy places and give them a firm place to stand.

Set my child's feet on the solid rock of Jesus Christ. Keep them from wobbling in weakness, and empower them to stand firm in strength.

The Knees: Relationship with God

> The eyes of the LORD search the whole earth in order to strengthen those whose hearts are fully committed to him. (2 Chronicles 16:9a NLT)

Lord, as Your eyes range throughout the earth to strengthen those whose hearts are fully committed to You, I pray they will rest on my child. Show them what it means to be fully committed to You, and empower them to make that a reality throughout life. As my child makes an effort to exercise faith regularly, strengthen their commitment to You wholly.

The Feet: The Path My Child Takes

> Walk with the wise and become wise, for a companion of fools suffers harm. (Proverbs 13:20)

Lastly, I pray my child will walk with the wise and grow wise. Protect them from falling in step with fools. I ask You to connect my child with those who walk in tandem with You. I pray all this in Jesus' name, amen.

Day 11

The Mind: What My Child Thinks About

> You were taught, with regard to your former way of life, to put off your old self, which is being corrupted by its deceitful desires; to be made new in the attitude of your minds; and to put on the new self, created to be like God in true righteousness and holiness. (Ephesians 4:22–24)

Heavenly Father, I pray my child will continually put off desires that meddle with their mind and tinker with their thoughts. I pray my child's mind will be renewed with the truth. Please align their thinking with Your thinking, their attitudes with Your attitudes, their thoughts with Your thoughts.

The Eyes: What My Child Looks At

> Look straight ahead, and fix your eyes on what lies before you. (Proverbs 4:25 NLT)

Lord, fix my child's eyes straight ahead, directly before You—on what You have called them to be and to do in life. I pray my child's eyes will not deviate to selfish desires or pressure from others but will stay focused on the path You have mapped out.

The Ears: Who and What My Child Listens To

> Jesus said to him, "Be gone, Satan! For it is written ..."
> (Matthew 4:10a ESV)

I pray my child will not listen to the enemy's accusations, temptations, or misleading suggestions but will follow Christ's example by rejecting Satan's lies and replacing them with the truth.

The Mouth: Words My Child Speaks

> The soothing tongue is a tree of life, but a perverse tongue
> crushes the spirit. (Proverbs 15:4)

I pray my child will speak words that are a tree of life from which wonderful fruit grows. I pray they will not use words to crush anyone's spirit, discourage anyone's dreams, or tear down anyone's character but to boost up someone's spirit, encourage someone's dreams, and build up someone's character.

The Neck: Decisions That Turn My Child's Head

> Who are those who fear the LORD? He will show them
> the path they should choose. (Psalm 25:12 NLT)

I pray my child will always honor, respect, and revere You as Lord—that they will make decisions that please You instead of those that impress others. I pray You will instruct my child in the way they should choose and that they will follow it.

The Shoulders: Burdens and Worries

> Cast all your anxiety on him because he cares for you.
> (1 Peter 5:7)

Whether it is schoolwork, peer pressure, social injustice, spiritual confusion, world events, family struggles, or the host of other concerns that weigh heavy on the youth of today, help my child to take the weight off their shoulders and place it on Yours. Help my child know that You care for their worries and concerns and always will. And today, I cast my anxiety concerning my child on Your shoulders because I know You care for me and mine.

The Heart: Who and What My Child Loves

> I pray that you, being rooted and established in love, may have power, together with all the Lord's holy people, to grasp how wide and long and high and deep is the love of Christ. (Ephesians 3:17b–18)

I pray my child will be rooted and established in a love that only comes from You. Even though it is difficult to fathom, I pray they will grasp how wide and long and high and deep Christ's love really is.

The Back: Physical and Spiritual Protection

> The angel of the LORD encamps around those who fear him, and he delivers them. (Psalm 34:7)

I pray the angel of the Lord will encamp around my child today. Protect them in the physical and spiritual realms. Defend them against any snares of the enemy that could trap, tempt, or trip them up along life's path. Deliver my child from anyone or anything that could cause harm.

The Arms: Health and Strength

> Do not grieve, for the joy of the LORD is your strength.
> (Nehemiah 8:10b)

Lord, when my child becomes discouraged or downhearted by the belief that everyone else is more popular, more athletic, more intelligent, or better looking, I pray that the joy of knowing You and being Your child will give them strength. Rather than focusing on what they think they don't have, bring to mind all that they do have. I pray the joy of the Lord will be their strength.

The Hands: Gifts and Talents

> The LORD will open the heavens, the storehouse of his bounty, to send rain on your land in season and to bless all the work of your hands. You will lend to many nations but will borrow from none. The LORD will make you the head, not the tail. If you pay attention to the commands of the LORD your God that I give you this day and carefully follow them, you will always be at the top, never at the bottom. (Deuteronomy 28:12–13)

Heavenly Father, place a desire in my child to pay attention to and follow Your commands. May they be securely positioned at the top, never at the bottom; at the head, not at the tail. Please, Lord, open the storehouse of Your bounty and rain down blessings on the work of their hands.

An inexplicable bond exists between a mother and her child. While the new life is being knit together in a mother's womb, her very blood is pumped from her heart to her child's.

The Ring Finger: Future Spouse

> Do not be conformed to this world, but be transformed by the renewing of your mind, so that you may prove what the will of God is, that which is good and acceptable and perfect. (Romans 12:2 NASB)

I pray my child's future spouse will not simply copy the behavior and customs of this world but will find and follow the path that You have planned for them. I pray they will not be a crowd follower but a confident leader. No matter what this world says about who or what this person should be and do, I pray my child's future spouse will find comfort in being the exact person You created them to be.

The Side: Influential Relationships

> Love each other with genuine affection, and take delight
> in honoring each other. (Romans 12:10 NLT)

Lord, I pray my child will love friends and family with genuine affection and take delight in honoring them. Show them how to honor others, giving them precedence and consideration above their own personal desires. I pray they will not mind playing second fiddle when a friend has the opportunity to play first chair.

Sexuality: Sexual Purity and Identity

> At the beginning of creation God "made them male
> and female." "For this reason a man will leave his father
> and mother and be united to his wife, and the two will
> become one flesh." So they are no longer two, but one
> flesh. (Mark 10:6–8)

Lord, Your Word tells us that You created humankind as male and female. I pray my child will never experience gender confusion but embrace the gender they were created to be.

The Legs: Stand for Godly Principles

> If you do not stand firm in your faith, you will not stand
> at all. (Isaiah 7:9b)

Help my child to stand firm in faith and not be swayed by the world's ways. Remind them that if we fail to stand firm on the truth, we risk setting ourselves up for a fall. I pray my child will not allow the criticism of others—whether it's from an online post or a debate at school—weaken their faith or stir up doubt about the truth of who You are.

The Knees: Relationship with God

> When pride comes, then comes disgrace, but with humility comes wisdom. (Proverbs 11:2)

I pray against any spirit of pride in my child's life that would cause them to have an attitude of self-importance and self-sufficiency. I pray against the false belief that we can make life work on our own, apart from You. Help my child to bend a knee in humility so that You can raise them up with honor.

The Feet: The Path My Child Takes

> My steps have stayed on your path; I have not wavered from following you. (Psalm 17:5 NLT)

Finally, I pray my child's feet will stay on the path You have marked out for them and that they will not waver from following You or deviate from Your plan. Guide my child's steps so that they will not slip on seductive sin but walk surefooted in constructive conviction. I pray all this in Jesus' name, amen.

Day 12

The Mind: What My Child Thinks About

> He [Jesus] opened their minds so they could understand
> the Scriptures. (Luke 24:45)

Heavenly Father, just as You opened the minds of the men in the New Testament to understand the Scriptures, I pray You will open my child's mind as well. I pray they will not be confused by the Scripture but enlightened by Your Word. Pull up the shades, open the shutters, turn on the lights! I pray You will help it all make sense.

The Eyes: What My Child Looks At

> A discerning person keeps wisdom in view, but a fool's
> eyes wander to the ends of the earth. (Proverbs 17:24)

Lord, I pray my child will be a wise person whose eyes do not wander toward anything or anyone impure or immoral. I pray their eyes will not wander to the ends of the earth, looking for a better way, a better truth, or a better life but that they will stay focused on Jesus—the only way, the only truth, and the only source of life.

The Ears: Who and What My Child Listens To

> Blessed are your eyes, because they see; and your ears, because they hear. (Matthew 13:16 NLT)

I pray my child will be blessed because they see You and hear You in everyday life

The Mouth: Words My Child Speaks

> The heart of the godly thinks carefully before speaking; the mouth of the wicked overflows with evil words. (Proverbs 15:28 NLT)

I pray my child will think carefully before speaking and not say the first words that pop in their head.

The Neck: Decisions That Turn My Child's Head

> Be kind and compassionate to one another, forgiving each other, just as in Christ God forgave you. (Ephesians 4:32)

Father, I pray my child will learn that forgiveness begins with a decision, not an emotion. I pray they will be quick to forgive, just as in Christ God has forgiven us. Help my child to never be bound by bitterness, wrapped in resentment, or hindered by hate.

The Shoulders: Burdens and Worries

> Do not be anxious about anything, but in every situation, by prayer and petition, with thanksgiving, present your

requests to God. And the peace of God, which transcends all understanding, will guard your hearts and your minds in Christ Jesus. (Philippians 4:6–7)

When my child feels weighed down with worry about friends, finances, family, acceptance, significance, or performance, I pray they will remember this truth: they are a child of God who has been given everything needed to succeed. I pray my child will not be anxious about anything but will pray about everything. May Your peace, which transcends all human understanding, guard their heart and mind so that they will not pick up those burdens and start worrying again.

The Heart: Who and What My Child Loves

You will seek me and find me when you seek me with all your heart. (Jeremiah 29:13)

I pray my child will seek You with their whole heart. Thank You for promising to be found when they do.

The Back: Physical and Spiritual Protection

He will cover you with his wings; you will be safe in his care; his faithfulness will protect and defend you. (Psalm 91:4 GNT)

Thank You, God, for Your protective presence. Cover my child as a mother hen protects her chicks, and shelter them with Your outstretched wings.

The Arms: Health and Strength

> David found strength in the LORD his God. (1 Samuel
> 30:6b NLT)

When my child is discouraged or disheartened and feels all alone, help them find strength in You. I pray my child will not depend on peers, people, possessions, or popularity to be lifted up and pulled out of a pit but will be strengthened by the truth of who they are in Christ: a chosen, holy, dearly loved child of God who is equipped by the Father, empowered by the Holy Spirit, and enveloped in Jesus Christ.

The Hands: Gifts and Talents

> Do you see someone skilled in their work? They will serve
> before kings. (Proverbs 22:29a)

I pray You will bless my child's mental and physical abilities in the present to prepare them to be a competent and successful adult in the future.

The Ring Finger: Future Spouse

> I found the one I love. (Song of Solomon 3:4b NKJV)

I pray my child's future spouse will be the one You have chosen. Keep both of them away from the wrong person. I pray the decision to marry will be very clear to both of them.

The Side: Influential Relationships

> Love is patient, love is kind. It does not envy, it does not
> boast, it is not proud. It does not dishonor others, it is not
> self-seeking, it is not easily angered, it keeps no record of

wrongs. Love does not delight in evil but rejoices with the truth. It always protects, always trusts, always hopes, always perseveres. (1 Corinthians 13:4–7)

I pray my child will be patient and kind with their family, friends, and those with whom they walk side by side. Show my child how to demonstrate a love that is not envious, boastful, proud, dishonoring, self-seeking, or easily angered. I pray they will not keep a record of wrongs but forgive quickly and completely. May they not delight when circumstances go wrong for others but celebrate when situations go right. Give them a love for family, friends, classmates, workmates, teammates, and eventually a forever-mate—a love that always protects, always trusts, always hopes, and always perseveres.

Sexuality: Sexual Purity and Identity

How can a young person stay on the path of purity? By living according to your word. (Psalm 119:9)

There are so many enticements that can lead young people off the path of purity. I pray my child will not be pulled off the path by violent video games, crude humor, foul language, blatant disrespect for authority, sexual experimentation, and mischievous misconduct to try to fit in. I pray they will stay on the right road even when friends take a detour.

The Legs: Stand for Godly Principles

Thanks be to God! He gives us the victory through our Lord Jesus Christ. Therefore, my dear brothers and sisters, stand firm. Let nothing move you. (1 Corinthians 15:57–58a)

God, thank You for giving us the victory over sin and death through Jesus Christ. I pray my child will stand firm on this truth and let no one—not peers, friends, teachers, or social media—undermine their courage, confidence, conviction, or commitment to Christ.

The Knees: Relationship with God

> The LORD mocks the mockers but is gracious to the humble. (Proverbs 3:34 NLT)

I pray my child will not be proud or arrogant but humble and grateful. Remove any sense of pride that would keep them from bending the knee, and remind them of the many ways You have heaped on undeserved grace.

The Feet: The Path My Child Takes

> Praise our God, all peoples, let the sound of his praise be heard; he has preserved our lives and kept our feet from slipping. (Psalm 66:8–9)

Finally, I pray You will keep my child's feet from slipping and make each step secure. Put a song on their lips and praise in their heart. I pray all this in Jesus' name, amen.

Day 13

The Mind: What My Child Thinks About

I keep asking that the God of our Lord Jesus Christ,
the glorious Father, may give you the Spirit of wisdom
and revelation, so that you may know him better.
(Ephesians 1:17)

Heavenly Father, I pray You will give my child the Spirit of wisdom and
revelation so that they may know You better—not just intellectually but
personally, intimately, and experientially.

The Eyes: What My Child Looks At

Lift up your eyes and look to the heavens: Who created
all these? He who brings out the starry host one by one
and calls forth each of them by name. Because of his great
power and mighty strength, not one of them is missing.
(Isaiah 40:26)

I pray my child will lift their eyes toward heaven and see Your great
power and mighty strength in all creation. Let them know that if You

can take care of the tiniest minutiae of heaven and the grandest balance of the universe, then you can take care of them today.

The Ears: Who and What My Child Listens To

> While he was still speaking, a bright cloud covered them, and a voice from the cloud said, "This is my Son, whom I love; with him I am well pleased. Listen to him!" (Matthew 17:5)

Whether my child is reading the Bible or listening to someone else read the words, I pray they will listen as though Jesus were speaking to them directly.

The Mouth: Words My Child Speaks

> Death and life are in the power of the tongue. (Proverbs 18:21a NASB)

I pray my child will use words to speak life to others. I pray they will use words to build up and not tear down, to encourage and not discourage, and to heal and not hurt.

The Neck: Decisions That Turn My Child's Head

> The way of fools seems right to them, but the wise listen to advice. (Proverbs 12:15)

When my child needs to make a major decision, I pray they will be open to receiving wise counsel. Help them avoid the pride of giving in to what seems right and, instead, be willing to listen to godly men and women who are older and wiser.

The Shoulders: Burdens and Worries

> I praise you because I am fearfully and wonderfully made;
> your works are wonderful, I know that full well. (Psalm
> 139:14)

I pray my child will not be dissatisfied with their outward appearance but content and confident in the masterpiece they truly are. Enable my child to always consider what's true: that the person they see in the mirror has been carefully, intentionally, and wonderfully made by a loving Creator.

The Heart: Who and What My Child Loves

> Create in me a clean heart, O God, and renew a right
> spirit within me. (Psalm 51:10 ESV)

Father, I know there is an all-out attack by the enemy of this world for the heart of my child. I pray against his wiles in the name of Jesus. I pray You will make my child's heart pure. Clean it up and clean it out by the power of Your Holy Spirit. Breathe a fresh anointing of Your Holy Spirit into my child's life today.

The Back: Physical and Spiritual Protection

> Though a thousand fall at your side, though ten thousand
> are dying around you, these evils will not touch you.
> (Psalm 91:7 NLT)

Lord, even though it may seem the world is falling apart around my child today, help them rest secure in Your protection and provision. Shield my child from danger, and rescue them from harm.

The Arms: Health and Strength

> She dresses herself with strength and makes her arms strong. (Proverbs 31:17 ESV)

I pray my child will be dressed with strength—with strong arms that are ready for any task they must accomplish today.

The Hands: Gifts and Talents

> Let us not become weary in doing good, for at the proper time we will reap a harvest if we do not give up. (Galatians 6:9)

Whenever my child feels like quitting, give them the stamina to press on with the knowledge that a harvest of benefits will be reaped at the proper time if they don't give up.

The Ring Finger: Future Spouse

> The LORD is a shelter for the oppressed, a refuge in times of trouble. Those who know your name trust in you, for you, O LORD, do not abandon those who search for you. (Psalm 9:9–10 NLT)

I pray my child's future spouse will learn how to work through life's difficulties so they will be ready to work through the struggles that come with every marriage. Help my child's future mate grow into a person who does not run away from adversity but holds tightly to You when the winds of calamity blow and the waves of uncertainty rage.

The Side: Influential Relationships

> [Jesus said,] A new commandment I give to you, that you
> love one another: just as I have loved you, you also are to
> love one another. (John 13:34 ESV)

I pray You will help my child learn how to love other people as Jesus loves them—sacrificially, unconditionally, and with a servant's heart.

Sexuality: Sexual Purity and Identity

> Can a man scoop fire into his lap without his clothes
> being burned? (Proverbs 6:27)

Lord, I know a man or woman cannot build a fire in their lap and not burn their pants. I pray my child will not toy with, trifle with, flirt with, or fiddle with anything that stirs up sexual urges or images that could have damaging consequences.

The Legs: Stand for Godly Principles

> Be on your guard; stand firm in the faith; be courageous;
> be strong. (1 Corinthians 16:13)

I pray my child will be alert and on guard against anyone or anything that would cause them to question faith in Jesus. Give them the strength and stamina to stand firm in faith through the ups and downs of life. I pray my child will continue to mature in faith to become a person of courage and confidence who does not buckle under pressure or temptation but stands firm on solid ground of truth.

The Knees: Relationship with God

> I am sure of this, that he who began a good work in you
> will bring it to completion at the day of Jesus Christ.
> (Philippians 1:6 ESV)

Father, I don't have the slightest doubt in my mind that You, who started this great work of redemption in my child's life, will bring them to maturity in the faith. I will join in the celebration of the completion of this process on the day of Christ's return!

The Feet: The Path My Child Takes

> Give careful thought to the paths for your feet and be
> steadfast in all your ways. Do not turn to the right or the
> left; keep your foot from evil. (Proverbs 4:26–27)

Finally, I pray my child will give careful thought to the path they take. May each step be safe, secure, and sure. Help my child not turn to the right or to the left but continue straight on the path You have marked out for them. I pray all this in Jesus' name, amen.

Day 14

The Mind: What My Child Thinks About

I pray that you, being rooted and established in love, may have power, together with all the Lord's holy people, to grasp how wide and long and high and deep is the love of Christ, and to know this love that surpasses knowledge—that you may be filled to the measure of all the fullness of God. (Ephesians 3:17b–19)

Father God, I pray my child will be deeply rooted and securely grounded in Your love. Take away any doubts about Your unfathomable love. Help them understand how wide and long and high and deep that love is even though it surpasses human comprehension. I pray my child will be able to grasp the extravagant dimensions of Your love—that they will experience the breadth, measure the length, plumb the depths, and rise to the heights. May my child know experientially and practically what they understand intellectually and spiritually. Fill my child to all the fullness of Your divine presence.

The Eyes: What My Child Looks At

You will see it with your own eyes and say, "Great is the LORD—even beyond the borders of Israel!" (Malachi 1:5)

I pray my child will see You at work in everyday life today. I pray they will see many manifestations of Your glory with their own eyes and say, "Great is the Lord who works in my life!"

The Ears: Who and What My Child Listens To

He [Satan] was a murderer from the beginning, not holding to the truth, for there is no truth in him. When he lies, he speaks his native language, for he is a liar and the father of lies. (John 8:44b)

I pray my child will be able to discern the enemy's lies from God's truth—that they will not listen to anything that does not line up with Scripture.

The Mouth: Words My Child Speaks

He who loves purity of heart and whose speech is gracious will have the king as his friend. (Proverbs 22:11 AMP)

I pray my child's speech will be gracious, as if every word were a gift freely given to someone. May they find favor in the sight of leaders and those in authority because of the gracious and wise ways they use their words.

The Neck: Decisions That Turn My Child's Head

If we confess our sins, he is faithful and just to forgive us our sins and to cleanse us from all unrighteousness. (1 John 1:9 ESV)

Just as forgiving others begins with a decision, forgiving ourselves also begins with a decision. I pray my child will take hold of the truth that if we confess our sins, You are faithful and just and will forgive our sins and cleanse us from all unrighteousness. I pray my child will believe this and will never be shackled by shame, wrought with regret, or grieved with guilt but will live free knowing their sins are forgiven. Help my child understand that there is no condemnation for those who are in Christ Jesus.

The Shoulders: Burdens and Worries

> We do not dare to classify or compare ourselves with some who commend themselves. When they measure themselves by themselves and compare themselves with themselves, they are not wise. (2 Corinthians 10:12)

I pray my child will not worry about the accomplishments of others— that they will not be caught up in classifying, comparing, and measuring self-worth with other people who brag about how important they are. I pray my child will understand that those who think they are smarter, better, or more attractive than others are comparing themselves with themselves, which just shows how silly they really are.

The Heart: Who and What My Child Loves

> The love of money is a root of all kinds of evil. Some people, eager for money, have wandered from the faith and pierced themselves with many griefs. (1 Timothy 6:10)

While money is not evil in itself, Your Word tells us that the love of money is a root of all kinds of evil. I pray my child will never let a desire for money or wealth come before a desire to please You. May they be a generous giver with an open hand and not a greedy miser with a tight fist.

The Back: Physical and Spiritual Protection

> He will command his angels concerning you to guard you in all your ways; they will lift you up in their hands, so that you will not strike your foot against a stone. (Psalm 91:11–12)

Loving Lord, thank You for Your angels who guard and protect my child wherever they go. I pray Your angels will lift up my child with their hands to catch them if they fall.

The Arms: Health and Strength

> Be strong in the Lord and in his mighty power. (Ephesians 6:10)

I pray my child will be strong in the Lord and in His mighty power. No matter what happens throughout the day, I pray they will remain firm in faith, uncompromising in convictions, and courageous in character.

The Hands: Gifts and Talents

> We are God's handiwork, created in Christ Jesus to do good works, which God prepared in advance for us to do. (Ephesians 2:10)

God has given
moms the privilege
and parental
responsibility to
shape and to mold
not just another
human being but an
eternal soul, for a very
short, very fleeting
period of time.

Help my child to understand that they are Your handiwork—Your masterpiece! We were each created in Christ Jesus to do good works, which You prepared in advance for us to do. As they mature and grow, I pray You will make clear Your purpose and plan for all the gifts and talents You have given them.

The Ring Finger: Future Spouse

> Do not be yoked together with unbelievers. For what do righteousness and wickedness have in common? Or what fellowship can light have with darkness? (2 Corinthians 6:14)

I pray my child will choose a mate who loves You with a sincere heart so that they will not become unequally yoked.

The Side: Influential Relationships

> If another believer sins against you, go privately and point out the offense. If the other person listens and confesses it, you have won that person back. (Matthew 18:15 NLT)

If someone offends my child or hurts their feelings today, I pray they will not discuss the matter with others but go to the offender directly and settle the issue quickly. Help my child resist the temptation to stir up trouble or ill feelings by talking to other people about the incident. Instead, fill them with mercy, wisdom, and grace—with a sincere desire to confront the person one on one to settle the matter quickly and peacefully.

Sexuality: Sexual Purity and Identity

> You are a garden locked up, my sister, my bride; you are
> a spring enclosed, a sealed fountain. (Song of Songs 4:12)

Prayer for a Daughter: I pray my daughter will be a locked-up garden until it's time to hand her husband the key.

Prayer for a Son: I pray my son will wait to possess the key to his own private garden until his wife presents it to him on his wedding night.

The Legs: Stand for Godly Principles

> It is God who makes both us and you stand firm in Christ.
> He anointed us, set his seal of ownership on us, and put
> his Spirit in our hearts as a deposit, guaranteeing what is
> to come. (2 Corinthians 1:21–22)

In this world, where so many children walk away from the faith once they leave home, I pray my child will stand firm in all that has been taught and continue the journey of maturing in Christ. Thank You that You have anointed them, setting Your seal of ownership on them, and putting Your Holy Spirit in them as a deposit or down payment of what is to come.

The Knees: Relationship with God

> God testified concerning him: "I have found David son
> of Jesse, a man after my own heart; he will do everything
> I want him to do." (Acts 13:22b)

I pray my child will be a person after Your own heart, who will do every-thing You want them to do.

The Feet: The Path My Child Takes

> Do not set foot on the path of the wicked or walk in the
> way of evildoers. Avoid it, do not travel on it; turn from it
> and go on your way. (Proverbs 4:14–15)

Lastly, I pray my child will not set foot on the path of the wicked or walk in the way of evildoers. I pray they will avoid it, turn from it, and not be enticed by it. Help my child stay on the path You have marked out for them. I pray all this in Jesus' name, amen.

Day 15

The Mind: What My Child Thinks About

"Who has understood the mind of the Lord so as to instruct him?" But we have the mind of Christ. (1 Corinthians 2:16 ESV)

Heavenly Father, Your ways are higher than our ways, and Your thoughts are higher than our thoughts—they are beyond human understanding. However, the Bible tells us that believers have the mind of Christ. I pray that as my child matures, they will align their thoughts with Christ's thoughts, their reasoning with Christ's reasoning, and their purpose with Christ's purposes.

The Eyes: What My Child Looks At

The eye is the lamp of the body. If your eyes are healthy, your whole body will be full of light. But if your eyes are unhealthy, your whole body will be full of darkness. (Matthew 6:22–23a)

Lord, Your Word tells us that the eye is the lamp of the body—that what we look at affects our entire being. I pray my child will have eyes wide open to all that turns up the light in their life and eyes shut tightly to all that would snuff it out.

The Ears: Who and What My Child Listens To

> [Jesus said,] My sheep listen to my voice; I know them, and they follow me. (John 10:27)

Jesus, thank You for shepherding my child today. I pray they will recognize and listen to Your voice as the sheep recognize and listen to the shepherd's voice. I pray my child will follow You and not wander away from the Shepherd.

The Mouth: Words My Child Speaks

> [There is] a time to be silent and a time to speak. (Ecclesiastes 3:7b)

I pray my child will know when to keep silent and when to speak up. I pray they will have a discerning spirit that knows when to open their mouth and when to keep it closed.

The Neck: Decisions That Turn My Child's Head

> He has removed our sins as far from us as the east is from the west. (Psalm 103:12 NLT)

When my child begins to feel guilty or ashamed over past sins You have already forgiven, help them remember that You have removed their sins as far as the east is from the west and that You remember forgiven sins no more.

The Shoulders: Burdens and Worries

> Pay careful attention to your own work, for then you will
> get the satisfaction of a job well done, and you won't need
> to compare yourself to anyone else. (Galatians 6:4 NLT)

I pray my child will pay careful attention to their own work and not worry about how well someone else is doing. I pray against the spirit of comparison that would open the door to self-imposed burdens and worries. Remove the burden of comparison with the knowledge of their uniqueness.

The Heart: Who and What My Child Loves

> Teach me your way, O LORD, that I may walk in your
> truth; unite my heart to fear your name. (Psalm 86:11 ESV)

Teach my child Your way so that they may walk in Your truth. Give my child an undivided heart, one that fears Your name. Keep them from being wishy-washy when it comes to faith but decidedly sure and wholly Yours.

The Back: Physical and Spiritual Protection

> The LORD will keep you from all harm—he will watch
> over your life; the LORD will watch over your coming and
> going both now and forevermore. (Psalm 121:7–8)

Lord, I pray You will keep my child from harm—that You will watch over their life and protect it. I pray You will guard my child's coming and going both now and forevermore.

The Arms: Health and Strength

> You then, my child, be strengthened by the grace that is
> in Christ Jesus. (2 Timothy 2:1 ESV)

Just as Paul prayed for Timothy, his son in the faith, I pray for the child of
my heart. I pray that they will be strengthened and empowered inwardly
and outwardly by the power of the gospel and the truth of grace that is
only found in Christ Jesus.

The Hands: Gifts and Talents

> Whatever you do, work at it with all your heart, as working
> for the Lord, not for human masters. (Colossians 3:23)

Whatever tasks my child tackles today, I pray they will do it with all
their heart, as if they were doing it for Jesus.

The Ring Finger: Future Spouse

> He [Jesus] got up from the meal, took off his outer cloth-
> ing, and wrapped a towel around his waist. After that, he
> poured water into a basin and began to wash his disciples'
> feet, drying them with the towel that was wrapped around
> him.… "Now that I, your Lord and Teacher, have washed
> your feet, you also should wash one another's feet." (John
> 13:4–5, 14)

I pray my child's future spouse will have a servant's heart. When my
child and their spouse marry, I pray they will serve each other as Jesus
modeled for us through his disciples.

The Side: Influential Relationships

> In everything, do to others what you would have them
> do to you, for this sums up the Law and the Prophets.
> (Matthew 7:12)

I pray my child will treat others the way they would like to be treated—with love, honor, and respect.

Sexuality: Sexual Purity and Identity

> Can he walk on hot coals and not blister his feet? (Proverbs
> 6:28 NLT)

I pray my child will remember that sex before marriage always has consequences, and none of them good. Help them to remember that it is not possible to walk on hot coals and not come away with blistered feet. Likewise, we cannot toy with temptation and not be plagued with guilt.

The Legs: Stand for Godly Principles

> It is for freedom that Christ has set us free. Stand firm,
> then, and do not let yourselves be burdened again by a
> yoke of slavery. (Galatians 5:1)

I pray my child will stand firm on the finished work of Jesus Christ. I pray they will live fully and free in Your mercy and grace. Keep my child from being burdened by religious rules and regulations that have nothing to do with a relationship with You. Protect them from falling into the trap of trying to earn what they already have in You.

The Knees: Relationship with God

> Pride goes before destruction, and a haughty spirit before
> a fall. (Proverbs 16:18 ESV)

I pray my child will not be prideful, haughty, or arrogant but that they will be humble, submissive, and malleable in Your hands. May their relationship with You be characterized by obedience that flows from a deep, abiding love.

The Feet: The Path My Child Takes

> This is what the LORD says: "Stand at the crossroads and
> look; ask for the ancient paths, ask where the good way
> is, and walk in it, and you will find rest for your souls."
> (Jeremiah 6:16a)

Finally, as my child stands at various crossroads—places where a decision to turn to the left or to the right must be made—open their eyes to see the footprints of godly men and women who have gone before, and give them clarity. Give my child the humility to ask for direction and wisdom when choosing the right path. Help them discover the rest for a weary soul that only comes from trusting Your way—and believing that it's the best way. I pray all this in Jesus' name, amen.

Day 16

The Mind: What My Child Thinks About

> One thing I do: Forgetting what is behind and straining toward what is ahead, I press on toward the goal to win the prize for which God has called me heavenward in Christ Jesus. (Philippians 3:13b–14)

Sovereign Lord, I pray my child will not get stuck dwelling on past mistakes but, instead, will learn the lessons and move on. I pray they will let go of past sins that bring shame, past offenses that bring bitterness, or missed opportunities that bring regret. I pray they will forget what lies behind and reach forward to what lies ahead. Help my child think about the exciting journey of becoming all You have created them to be, pursuing all You have planned for them to do.

The Eyes: What My Child Looks At

> Blessed are your eyes because they see, and your ears because they hear. (Matthew 13:16)

I pray my child's eyes will be blessed—seeing You at work in every detail of life today.

The Ears: Who and What My Child Listens To

> Obscene stories, foolish talk, and coarse jokes—these are
> not for you. (Ephesians 5:4a NLT)

I pray my child will not listen to obscene stories, foolish talk, or coarse jokes. Give them the courage to walk away, turn it off, or shut it down. I pray my child will not allow impure thoughts to enter their mind through the portal of their ears.

The Mouth: Words My Child Speaks

> Words from the mouth of the wise are gracious, but fools
> are consumed by their own lips. (Ecclesiastes 10:12)

I pray my child's words will be wise and gracious. I pray they will not use destructive words that will blow up and bite back but use gracious words that impart peace and bring blessings.

The Neck: Decisions That Turn My Child's Head

> Teach me knowledge and good judgment, for I trust your
> commands. (Psalm 119:66)

God of all wisdom, as my child grows and matures, I pray You will teach them knowledge and good judgment so that they will make decisions that honor and glorify You.

The Shoulders: Burdens and Worries

> I am convinced that neither death nor life, neither angels
> nor demons, neither the present nor the future, nor any

powers, neither height nor depth, nor anything else in all creation, will be able to separate us from the love of God that is in Christ Jesus our Lord. (Romans 8:38–39)

I pray my child will never worry that You will stop loving or caring about them because of past actions, words, or thoughts. May they be convinced that neither death nor life, neither angels nor demons, neither the present nor the future, nor any powers, neither height nor depth, nor anything else in all creation, will be able to separate them from Your love.

Prayer is simply opening the storehouse of heaven for lavish blessings He wants to give.

The Heart: Who and What My Child Loves

Do not let my heart be drawn to what is evil so that I take part in wicked deeds along with those who are evildoers; do not let me eat their delicacies. (Psalm 141:4)

Shield my child's heart from being drawn toward the deeds of evildoers and wicked men, and lead them toward good works and godly people. Shield my child from envying the enticing delicacies of sin and encourage them to feast on the fruit of a pure heart and godly living.

The Back: Physical and Spiritual Protection

> You hem me in behind and before, and you lay your hand upon me. (Psalm 139:5)

Almighty God, I pray You will hem my child in today—that You surround them as if they were sewn into the hem of Your garment. Be a shield before my child and a bulwark behind. Thank You for the assurance that there is no place they can go that is out of Your protective reach.

The Arms: Health and Strength

> Wait for the LORD; be strong and take heart and wait for the LORD. (Psalm 27:14)

I pray my child will wait for You, hope in You, and expect great things from You, that they will not quit when times get tough but take heart and move forward in the power of the Holy Spirit. Give my child strength for the journey and power for the task.

The Hands: Gifts and Talents

> Lazy people want much but get little, but those who work hard will prosper. (Proverbs 13:4 NLT)

I pray my child will not be a lazy person who wants much but gets little but instead be a hard worker who is diligent and prosperous.

The Ring Finger: Future Spouse

Two are better than one, because they have a good return for their labor: If either of them falls down, one can help the other up. But pity anyone who falls and has no one to help them up. Also, if two lie down together, they will keep warm. But how can one keep warm alone? Though one may be overpowered, two can defend themselves. A cord of three strands is not quickly broken. (Ecclesiastes 4:9–12)

Lord, I pray You will lead my child to a future spouse who will support them during difficult days. I pray they will work together to help each other succeed in love and in life. May they never have any sense of competition, contention, or one-upmanship. Show them how to live in unity as husband and wife as You intended. May they be a tightly braided cord of three strands intertwined with You.

The Side: Influential Relationships

Do not judge others, and you will not be judged. For you will be treated as you treat others. The standard you use in judging is the standard by which you will be judged. And why worry about a speck in your friend's eye when you have a log in your own? How can you think of saying to your friend, "Let me help you get rid of that speck in your eye," when you can't see past the log in your own eye? Hypocrite! First get rid of the log in your own eye; then you will see well enough to deal with the speck in your friend's eye. (Matthew 7:1–5 NLT)

Help my child resist the temptation to judge, criticize, or condemn others so that they will not be judged, criticized, or condemned in return. Make them aware of the plank in their own eye before attempting to take the speck from someone else's. Rather than pointing out the other's faults, help them work on correcting their own faults and strengthening their own weaknesses. May my child make an effort to look inward rather than outward at others.

Sexuality: Sexual Purity and Identity

God created mankind in his own image, in the image of
God he created them; male and female he created them.
(Genesis 1:27)

Prayer for a Daughter: I pray my daughter will know she was created in the image of God, that God fashioned her to be a female who reflects You in all she does. I pray against any gender identity confusion or culture-driven delusion. May she celebrate her femaleness with confidence.

Prayer for a Son: I pray my son will know he was created in the image of God, that God fashioned him to be a male who reflects You in all he does. I pray against any gender confusion or culture-driven delusion. May he celebrate his maleness with confidence.

The Legs: Stand for Godly Principles

He alone is my rock and my salvation, my fortress where
I will not be shaken. (Psalm 62:6 NLT)

Lord, our Rock and our Salvation, help my child stand firm in faith and strong in convictions. I pray they will not be shot down, shaken up, or snuffed out by the schemes of the enemy. Strengthen their resolve, making their faith immovable.

The Knees: Relationship with God

> God has highly exalted him and bestowed on him the name that is above every name, so that at the name of Jesus every knee should bow, in heaven and on earth and under the earth, and every tongue confess that Jesus Christ is Lord, to the glory of God the Father. (Philippians 2:9–11 ESV)

I pray my child's knee will bow and their tongue confess that Jesus Christ is Lord. As they grow physically, I pray they will mature spiritually.

The Feet: The Path My Child Takes

> This God is our God for ever and ever; he will be our guide even to the end. (Psalm 48:14)

Finally, eternal God, guide my child's every step. Shine your light to illumine the dark places, and extend Your hand to assist in the uncertain spaces. Thank You for leading my child all the days of their life. I pray all this in Jesus' name, amen.

Day 17

The Mind: What My Child Thinks About

Examine me, LORD, and put me to the test; refine my mind and my heart. For Your goodness is before my eyes, and I have walked in Your truth. (Psalm 26:2–3 NASB)

Heavenly Father, I pray You will examine my child's mind to root out any thoughts that would tempt them to walk contrary to Your truth. I pray against any lies of the enemy that would sneak into my child's mind and cause doubt.

The Eyes: What My Child Looks At

Watch and pray so that you will not fall into temptation. The spirit is willing, but the flesh is weak. (Matthew 26:41)

I pray my child will watch and pray so that they will not fall into temptation. I pray they give attention to what and who they look at. I pray against the schemes of the devil to try and entice my child with tempting images from the host of media outlets. Strengthen them spiritually to resist temptation confidently.

The Ears: Who and What My Child Listens To

> The time will come when people will not put up with sound doctrine. Instead, to suit their own desires, they will gather around them a great number of teachers to say what their itching ears want to hear. They will turn their ears away from the truth and turn aside to myths. (2 Timothy 4:3–4)

I pray my child will not listen to those who twist the truth to make it say what they want it to say. I pray they will not listen to anyone who misinterprets Scripture to suit specific personal agendas and desires but listen to those who stick to truth. I pray my child will not be drawn to ear-tickling teachers who sell the gospel to get what they want or be confused by those whose ideas of right and wrong change with the seasons.

The Mouth: Words My Child Speaks

> I tell you that everyone will have to give account on the day of judgment for every empty word they have spoken. For by your words you will be acquitted, and by your words you will be condemned. (Matthew 12:36–37)

I pray my child will be careful of the words they speak, remembering that we will all have to give account on the day of judgment for every empty, careless word spoken. I pray my child will be mindful of the power of words to affect their life and the lives of others.

The Neck: Decisions That Turn My Child's Head

> Teach me to do your will, for you are my God. May your gracious Spirit lead me forward on a firm footing. (Psalm 143:10 NLT)

I pray You will show my child the best choice for every decision they have to make today. Provide the knowledge of Your will so that they will be able to evaluate options wisely and choose Your best confidently. May Your Holy Spirit lead them forward on the firm footing of right choices.

The Shoulders: Burdens and Worries

> We know that in all things God works for the good of those who love him, who have been called according to his purpose. (Romans 8:28)

When my child is brokenhearted by disappointment, I pray they will believe that You work all things out for their good in Your own time. Help them not to get stuck in a difficult moment but to move forward, knowing You have a plan.

The Heart: Who and What My Child Loves

> I say, love your enemies! Pray for those who persecute you! (Matthew 5:44 NLT)

Lord, soften my child's heart to love their enemies and pray for those who persecute them. Protect my child's heart from becoming bitter or resentful, and fill it with mercy and grace.

The Back: Physical and Spiritual Protection

> Having disarmed the powers and authorities, he made a public spectacle of them, triumphing over them by the cross. (Colossians 2:15)

Lord, I stand on the promise that the devil has no authority over my child because You have disarmed the spiritual powers and authorities of evil, made a public spectacle of them in the heavenlies, and triumphed over them by the cross. I pray You will protect my child from the enemy's attempt to retake any conquered ground. I praise You for the assurance that greater is Jesus, who reigns in my child, than the defeated devil that is in the world (1 John 4:4).

The Arms: Health and Strength

> The LORD is my strength and my shield; my heart trusts in him, and he helps me. My heart leaps for joy, and with my song I praise him. (Psalm 28:7)

Heavenly Father, thank You for being my child's immeasurable strength and impenetrable shield. As they grow and mature, I pray they will have a deeper understanding of what that means. No matter what they face today, I pray for strength and a deeper trust in You.

The Hands: Gifts and Talents

> Everyone who competes in the games goes into strict training. They do it to get a crown that will not last, but we do it to get a crown that will last forever. Therefore I do not run like someone running aimlessly; I do not fight like a boxer beating the air. (1 Corinthians 9:25–26)

I pray my child will work hard to develop the skills You have given. I ask that You give discipline to apply themselves in school now so they will have a successful vocation in the future. Help my child see that work now will bring rewards later.

The Ring Finger: Future Spouse

> "I hate divorce!" says the LORD, the God of Israel. "To divorce your wife is to overwhelm her with cruelty," says the LORD of Heaven's Armies. "So guard your heart; do not be unfaithful to your wife." (Malachi 2:16 NLT)

Father, I pray against the spirit of divorce so prevalent in our culture. I know You hate divorce—the violent dismembering of the "one flesh" of marriage. I pray my child and future spouse will work through difficulties and not give up when they disagree. May they both be on guard to protect their marriage vows. Help them not tear apart what You have joined together.

The Side: Influential Relationships

> Though one may be overpowered, two can defend themselves. A cord of three strands is not quickly broken. (Ecclesiastes 4:12)

I pray You will give my child at least one good friend who will stick with them through thick and thin. May my child have a godly ally with whom they can form a strong bond—a three-stranded bond with Jesus at the core.

Sexuality: Sexual Purity and Identity

> God's will is for you to be holy, so stay away from all sexual sin. Then each of you will control his own body

and live in holiness and honor—not in lustful passion like the pagans who do not know God and his ways. (1 Thessalonians 4:3–5 NLT)

Lord, I declare and proclaim that my child will be set apart for holy use—that they will control passions and stay away from all sexual sin. I pray against peer pressure that would try to lead them astray, and I pray for godly friends who will encourage godly character.

The Legs: Stand for Godly Principles

Speak up for those who cannot speak for themselves, for the rights of all who are destitute. Speak up and judge fairly; defend the rights of the poor and needy. (Proverbs 31:8–9)

I pray my child will stand up for those who cannot stand up for themselves, that they will speak up for those who cannot speak for themselves and defend those who cannot defend themselves. I pray they will stand up for those who are bullied or teased, to help them feel included and accepted.

The Knees: Relationship with God

Humble yourselves before the Lord, and he will lift you up. (James 4:10)

I pray my child will be humble before You so that You will lift them up at the appointed time. Help my child resist the urge to brag or boast but to instead remain humble, knowing every ability to succeed comes from You.

The Feet: The Path My Child Takes

> We are always of good courage. We know that while we
> are at home in the body we are away from the Lord, for
> we walk by faith, not by sight. (2 Corinthians 5:6–7 ESV)

Finally, help my child know what it means to walk by faith and not by
sight. Show them that there is more to this life than what can be seen
with physical eyes. Help my child trust in, believe in, and cling to the
truth of Your Word, regardless of present circumstances. May faith in
Your truth be their North Star as they navigate through life. I pray all
this in Jesus' name, amen.

Day 18

The Mind: What My Child Thinks About

> My goal is that they may be encouraged in heart and united in love, so that they may have the full riches of complete understanding, in order that they may know the mystery of God, namely, Christ, in whom are hidden all the treasures of wisdom and knowledge. (Colossians 2:2–3)

I pray my child will have the full riches of complete understanding to know the mystery of God, namely, Christ, in whom are hidden all the treasures of wisdom and knowledge. I pray You will open my child's mind to comprehend the vast richness of knowing Jesus and that You will deposit priceless wisdom and understanding into the vault of their mind. This sounds like a big request, but I know the deposits begin early and continue until the day we die.

The Eyes: What My Child Looks At

> "What do you want me to do for you?" Jesus asked him. The blind man said, "Rabbi, I want to see." (Mark 10:51)

Lord, just as the blind man wanted to see physically, I pray my child will want to see spiritually.

The Ears: Who and What My Child Listens To

> Everyone should be quick to listen, slow to speak and slow to become angry. (James 1:19b)

I pray my child will be quick to listen, slow to speak, and slow to become angry. I pray they will lead with the ears and follow with their mouth.

The Mouth: Words My Child Speaks

> Jesus called the crowd to him and said, "Listen and understand. What goes into someone's mouth does not defile them, but what comes out of their mouth, that is what defiles them." (Matthew 15:10–11)

I pray my child will understand that the words that come out of the mouth are just as important as the food that goes into the mouth. I pray they will not taint or tarnish their reputation with careless words but instead will choose words that represent Christ well.

The Neck: Decisions That Turn My Child's Head

> The fear of the LORD is the beginning of knowledge, but fools despise wisdom and instruction. (Proverbs 1:7)

I pray my child will make decisions based on a reverent fear and humble respect for Your sovereignty and perfect plan. Stir up a desire in them to seek Your wisdom for every decision and Your direction for every choice. I pray my child will not depend on worldly knowledge, with its human limitations, but on Your infinite wisdom, which knows no bounds.

> Prayer is the conduit through which God's power is released and His will is brought to earth as it is in heaven.

The Shoulders: Burdens and Worries

> If we confess our sins, he is faithful and just and will forgive us our sins and purify us from all unrighteousness. (1 John 1:9)

Help my child to know there is no sin any of us could ever commit that is beyond Your forgiveness. I pray they will confess quickly and repent wholeheartedly to be cleansed completely.

The Heart: Who and What My Child Loves

> Turn my heart toward your statutes and not toward self-
> ish gain. (Psalm 119:36)

Lord, please turn my child's heart toward loving You and Your ways rather than selfish gain.

The Back: Physical and Spiritual Protection

> The Lord is faithful, and he will strengthen you and pro-
> tect you from the evil one. (2 Thessalonians 3:3)

Lord, thank You for being faithful to strengthen and protect my child from the evil one today.

The Arms: Health and Strength

> Dear friend, I hope all is well with you and that you are
> as healthy in body as you are strong in spirit. (3 John
> 1:2 NLT)

I pray my child will be healthy in body and strong in spirit. Protect them from physical sickness and disease and spiritual weakness and waywardness.

The Hands: Gifts and Talents

> Make it your goal to live a quiet life, minding your
> own business and working with your hands, just as we
> instructed you before. Then people who are not believers

will respect the way you live, and you will not need to depend on others. (1 Thessalonians 4:11–12 NLT)

I pray my child will be disciplined in studies now so that they will be able to earn a living in the future without having to depend on others.

The Ring Finger: Future Spouse

The angel of the LORD encamps around those who fear him, and he delivers them. (Psalm 34:7)

I pray the angel of the Lord will encamp around my child's future spouse today. Protect this person in the physical and spiritual realms, defending against any snares of the enemy that could trap, tempt, or trip them. Deliver my child's future spouse from anyone or anything that could cause harm.

The Side: Influential Relationships

Accept one another, then, just as Christ accepted you, in order to bring praise to God. (Romans 15:7)

Lord, help my child accept those with whom they walk side by side, just as Christ accepts each one of us—totally and unconditionally.

Sexuality: Sexual Purity and Identity

Joseph was well-built and handsome, and after a while his master's wife took notice of Joseph and said, "Come to bed with me!" But he refused.… "How then could I do such a wicked thing and sin against God?" (Genesis 39:6b–8a, 9b)

I pray my child will be like young Joseph, who resisted sexual temptation and ran in the opposite direction. I pray they will consider sexual sin as more than just crossing a line or breaking a rule but recognize it as an offense against You.

The Legs: Stand for Godly Principles

Learn to do right; seek justice. Defend the oppressed. Take up the cause of the fatherless; plead the case of the widow. (Isaiah 1:17)

I pray my child will learn to do right to those who are treated wrong and seek justice for those who are treated unfairly. I pray they will stand up for the put down, reach out to the rejected, raise up the picked on, and befriend the bullied.

The Knees: Relationship with God

After Uzziah became powerful, his pride led to his downfall. (2 Chronicles 26:16a)

Oh Lord, as I have prayed for my child to be successful in life, I also pray against prideful thinking: the lie that our accomplishments are a result of our own hard work and talent. May my child always bend the knee in humility, gratitude, and awe of Your blessings—giving You the glory when anyone asks.

Feet: The Path My Child Takes

At one time you were darkness, but now you are light in
the Lord. Walk as children of light. (Ephesians 5:8 ESV)

Finally, I pray my child will walk as a child of light—that they will not
walk as one who doesn't know Christ but as one who does. May their
steps be good, right, and true. In Jesus' name, amen.

Day 19

The Mind: What My Child Thinks About

See to it that no one takes you captive through hollow and deceptive philosophy, which depends on human tradition and the elemental spiritual forces of this world rather than on Christ. (Colossians 2:8)

All-knowing, all-wise God, I pray no one will take my child's mind captive though intellectual arguments, human reasoning, or scientific theories, especially through social media and scholastic studies. I pray You will protect my child's mind from the trickery of human philosophy to erase the divine and explain away the truth. I pray against anything or anyone that tries to eradicate the truths of Scripture with man-made ideas.

The Eyes: What My Child Looks At

He entered Jericho and was passing through. And behold, there was a man named Zacchaeus. He was a chief tax collector and was rich. And he was seeking to see who Jesus was, but on account of the crowd he could not, because he was small in stature. So he ran on ahead and

climbed up into a sycamore tree to see him, for he was
about to pass that way. (Luke 19:1–4 ESV)

Just as Zacchaeus determinedly climbed the sycamore tree to see Jesus,
I pray my child will tenaciously do whatever it takes to see You clearly.

The Ears: Who and What My Child Listens To

Today you have acknowledged the LORD as your God;
you have promised to obey him, to keep all his laws, and
to do all that he commands. (Deuteronomy 26:17 GNT)

I pray my child will be committed to listening to Your voice speaking to
their heart and turn away from any voices of this world, the flesh, or the
devil that would lead them astray.

The Mouth: Words My Child Speaks

Instead, speaking the truth in love, we will grow to
become in every respect the mature body of him who is
the head, that is, Christ. (Ephesians 4:15)

I pray my child's words will be wrapped in a blanket of Your love. If a
friend, a family member, or a classmate must be confronted, I pray my
child will sift words through the sieve of mercy and grace. I pray they
will continue to mature in Christ and grow into the godly person You
have created them to be.

The Neck: Decisions That Turn My Child's Head

The LORD gives wisdom; from his mouth come knowledge and understanding. (Proverbs 2:6)

Father, give my child the wisdom, knowledge, and understanding needed to make godly decisions. Keep the world, the flesh, the devil—peer pressure, social media, or the urge to elevate self—from turning their head toward harmful choices.

The Shoulders: Burdens and Worries

> The LORD is close to the brokenhearted and saves those who are crushed in spirit. (Psalm 34:18)

Lord, thank You for being close to my child when they are brokenhearted and crushed in spirit. I pray You will lift them up when disappointment crashes in, bringing to mind the many reasons they have to be thankful.

The Heart: Who and What My Child Loves

> Above all else, guard your heart, for everything you do flows from it. (Proverbs 4:23)

Guard my child's heart against temptation. May they keep watch over it with the vigilance of a security guard at Fort Knox. Yes, Lord, I pray my child will guard their heart because everything else flows from it.

The Back: Physical and Spiritual Protection

> We know that God's children do not make a practice of sinning, for God's Son holds them securely, and the evil one cannot touch them. (1 John 5:18 NLT)

God, thank You for the assurance that Jesus holds my child securely in His hands today. I stand on the promise that the evil one cannot touch my child.

Thank You that nothing and no one can snatch them out of Your hand
[John 10:29]. I lay claim to those promises of protection for my child today.

The Arms: Health and Strength

> The LORD will guide you continually and satisfy your
> desire in scorched places and make your bones strong;
> and you shall be like a watered garden, like a spring of
> water, whose waters do not fail. (Isaiah 58:11 ESV)

Lord, thank You for always guiding my child and providing for their
needs. I pray they will be like a well-watered garden, like a spring whose
waters never fail.

The Hands: Gifts and Talents

> All hard work brings a profit, but mere talk leads only to
> poverty. The wealth of the wise is their crown, but the
> folly of fools yields folly. (Proverbs 14:23–24)

I pray my child will not be lazy but diligent to develop God-given talents
and abilities.

The Ring Finger: Future Spouse

> Run from sexual sin! No other sin so clearly affects the
> body as this one does. For sexual immorality is a sin
> against your own body. (1 Corinthians 6:18 NLT)

I pray my child's future spouse will flee sexual immorality and choose
to remain pure until marriage. When they are tempted to look at

sexually suggestive images or engage in immoral behavior, I pray they will have the conviction and courage to run in the opposite direction. Give them the self-confidence and self-control to go against the flow of the culture that values sex so little and the self-assurance and self-awareness that it will be worth the wait.

The Side: Influential Relationships

"Don't sin by letting anger control you." Don't let the sun go down while you are still angry, for anger gives a foothold to the devil. (Ephesians 4:26–27 NLT)

When my child gets upset or angry with anyone, soften their heart to seek prompt resolution. Help them to not go to bed angry, even if the issue is not resolved completely. Keep them from allowing anger to take control by holding a grudge, plotting revenge, replaying the offense, or refusing to let it go. Don't allow my child to give the devil a foothold through anger, bitterness, or unforgiveness.

Sexuality: Sexual Purity and Identity

She saw that the tree was beautiful, and its fruit looked delicious, and she wanted the wisdom it would give her. So she took some of the fruit and ate it. Then she gave some to her husband, who was with her, and he ate it, too. At that moment their eyes were opened, and they suddenly felt shame at their nakedness. So they sewed fig leaves together to cover themselves. (Genesis 3:6b–7 NLT)

Lord, I know that almost all sin follows these three steps seen in the garden of Eden: she saw, she wanted, she took. I pray my child will stop the downward spiral of sexual temptation at the first step. Even though they might see, I pray they will not want and will not take.

The Legs: Stand for Godly Principles

> David said to the Philistine, "You come against me with sword and spear and javelin, but I come against you in the name of the LORD Almighty, the God of the armies of Israel, whom you have defied." (1 Samuel 17:45)

Just as David took his stand against Goliath, I pray my child will take a stand against the enemies of the Lord Almighty, the God of the armies of Israel. May my child have the courage, confidence, and conviction to face the giants of this world.

The Knees: Relationship with God

> There is one God and one mediator between God and mankind, the man Christ Jesus, who gave himself as a ransom for all people. (1 Timothy 2:5–6a)

I pray my child will know there is one God and one mediator between God and mankind—Jesus, who gave himself as a ransom for all people. As they go through life, I know there will be others claiming there are many roads that lead to God. I pray they will not waver in the knowledge of the truth. May their relationship with You be so strong they will see the holes in any other religion quickly and clearly.

The Feet: The Path My Child Takes

> Calling the crowd to join his disciples, he [Jesus] said, "If any of you wants to be my follower, you must give up your own way, take up your cross, and follow me." (Mark 8:34 NLT)

Lastly, I pray my child will follow You all the days of their life. I pray my child will give up selfish desires that don't align with Your designed destiny and take hold of the path You have marked out for them. May they be willing to take up the cross and follow You, no matter the consequences. I pray all this in Jesus' name, amen.

Day 20

The Mind: What My Child Thinks About

For this reason, since the day we heard about you, we have not stopped praying for you. We continually ask God to fill you with the knowledge of his will through all the wisdom and understanding that the Spirit gives. (Colossians 1:9)

Dear Lord, I will never stop praying for my child. I pray You will fill them with the knowledge of Your will through spiritual wisdom and understanding that the world cannot give. I pray they will have spiritual wisdom that goes beyond human explanation and spiritual understanding that exceeds earthly education.

The Eyes: What My Child Looks At

Blessed are your eyes because they see, and your ears because they hear. (Matthew 13:16)

I pray my child will be blessed because their eyes have seen You and their ears have heard You.

The Ears: Who and What My Child Listens To

Samuel said [to God], "Speak, for your servant is listening."
(1 Samuel 3:10b)

I pray my child will be like young Samuel, who said, "Speak, for your servant is listening." I pray they will recognize and respond to Your voice speaking to their heart.

The Mouth: Words My Child Speaks

Nor should there be any obscenity, foolish talk or coarse joking, which are out of place, but rather thanksgiving. (Ephesians 5:4)

I pray my child will refrain from foolish talk, coarse joking, cursing, or swearing. I pray they will be so fluent in thanksgiving that others will want to know just what they have to be so happy about.

The Neck: Decisions That Turn My Child's Head

Trust in the LORD with all your heart and do not lean on your own understanding. In all your ways acknowledge Him, and He will make your paths straight. (Proverbs 3:5–6 NASB)

I pray my child will trust in You with their whole heart and not depend on human understanding—that they will acknowledge You and consult You before making any major decisions. Clear up any confusion that clouds their thinking, and clear away any fog that makes Your way difficult to see.

The Shoulders: Burdens and Worries

> As pressure and stress bear down on me, I find joy in your
> commands. (Psalm 119:143 NLT)

When pressure and stress bear down on my child, when the stress and strain of growing up feels too much for them to bear, help my child find joy in knowing You. May they understand that following godly principles is not meant to make life harder but to make life easier. Help them find joy in Your commands that offer instruction on how to have the best life possible.

The Heart: Who and What My Child Loves

> A heart at peace gives life to the body, but envy rots the
> bones. (Proverbs 14:30)

I pray my child will have a peaceful heart that gives life to the whole body—a healthy mind, a strong body, and stable emotions—rather than a stress-filled heart that leads to a host of physical, emotional, and mental ills. I pray my child will not allow envy to creep into their heart but be thankful for all the ways You have blessed them.

The Back: Physical and Spiritual Protection

> In that coming day no weapon turned against you will
> succeed. You will silence every voice raised up to accuse
> you. These benefits are enjoyed by the servants of the
> LORD; their vindication will come from me. I, the LORD,
> have spoken! (Isaiah 54:17 NLT)

Lord, I pray no weapon formed against my child will succeed. May You silence every voice raised up to falsely accuse them. I stand on the promise that these are benefits enjoyed by the servants of the Lord, which I am believing by faith that my child is and will forever be.

> # When we pray the Word of God, we pray the will of God.

The Arms: Health and Strength

> He gives strength to the weary and increases the power of the weak. Even youths grow tired and weary, and young men stumble and fall; but those who hope in the LORD will renew their strength. They will soar on wings like eagles; they will run and not grow weary, they will walk and not be faint. (Isaiah 40:29–31)

Lord, when my child gets tired and weary, whether it is emotionally, spiritually, mentally, or physically, give them the strength to continue moving forward and pressing on. Show them how to soar on wings like eagles that drift along on the current You provide rather than flapping ferociously to stay in flight. Help them to run and not grow weary, to walk and not be faint.

The Hands: Gifts and Talents

Scripture and Prayer for a Daughter: She sets about her work vigorously; her arms are strong for her tasks. (Proverbs 31:17)

I pray my daughter will be like the Proverbs 31 woman, who sets about her work vigorously and whose arms are strong for her tasks.

Scripture and Prayer for a Son: One of the servants answered, "I have seen a son of Jesse of Bethlehem who knows how to play the lyre. He is a brave man and a warrior. He speaks well and is a fine-looking man. And the LORD is with him." (1 Samuel 16:18)

I pray my son will be like the boy David, who polished the talents You gave him, practiced the skills You instilled in him, and represented You well to those who observed him.

The Ring Finger: Future Spouse

There the child grew up healthy and strong. He was filled with wisdom, and God's favor was on him. (Luke 2:40 NLT)

I pray my child's future spouse will grow up healthy and strong and that they will be filled with wisdom and God's favor.

The Side: Influential Relationships

> Carry each other's burdens, and in this way you will ful-
> fill the law of Christ. (Galatians 6:2)

I pray my child will have a heart to help friends and family when their
burden is too heavy to bear alone. Prompt them to lend a helping hand,
offer an encouraging word, or reach out with a caring heart. Teach them
how to be Jesus' hands and feet to others.

Sexuality: Sexual Purity and Identity

> Run from anything that stimulates youthful lusts.
> Instead, pursue righteous living, faithfulness, love, and
> peace. (2 Timothy 2:22a NLT)

Give my child the courage to run away from anything that stimulates
youthful lusts. Instead, I pray they will pursue righteousness, faithfulness, love, and peace.

The Legs: Stand for Godly Principles

> The righteous care about justice for the poor, but the
> wicked have no such concern. (Proverbs 29:7)

Lord, I pray my child would not be concerned only about what is
going on in their own small world but also in the world at large.
Help them to care about justice for the poor and the disenfranchised.
I pray my child will stand up for those who cannot stand up for
themselves.

The Knees: Relationship with God

Come close to God and He will come close to you. (James 4:8a NASB)

I pray my child will start their day in communion with You, continue each day in union with You, and end each day with thanksgiving to You. I pray they will draw near to You so that You will draw near to them.

The Feet: The Path My Child Takes

As Jesus went on from there, he saw a man named Matthew sitting at the tax collector's booth. "Follow me," he told him, and Matthew got up and followed him. (Matthew 9:9)

Finally, I pray my child will follow You all the days of their life. I pray they will respond to Jesus' invitation as Matthew did—quickly, completely, wholeheartedly. I pray all this in Jesus' name, amen.

Day 21

The Mind: What My Child Thinks About

> Set your minds on things above, not on earthly things.
> (Colossians 3:2)

Heavenly Father, I pray my child will set their mind on things above and not on earthly things below. I pray they will keep the revolving pinwheel of thoughts spinning on the axis of spiritual truth.

The Eyes: What My Child Looks At

> As they talked and discussed these things with each other, Jesus himself came up and walked along with them; but they were kept from recognizing him.... Then their eyes were opened and they recognized him, and he disappeared from their sight. (Luke 24:15–16, 31)

Lord, just as You opened the eyes of the men who walked with Jesus on the road to Emmaus, I pray You will open my child's eyes to see You walking right alongside them on the road of life.

The Ears: Who and What My Child Listens To

> The LORD … takes the upright into his confidence.
> (Proverbs 3:32b)

I pray my child will have such a personal, intimate relationship with You that You will share Your secrets with them. I pray they will lean into You like an intimate friend and listen to Your still, small voice speaking to their heart.

The Mouth: Words My Child Speaks

> Those who guard their mouths and their tongues keep themselves from calamity. (Proverbs 21:23)

I pray my child will guard their mouth and hold their tongue so that they will not say something they would later regret.

The Neck: Decisions That Turn My Child's Head

> Call to me and I will answer you and tell you great and unsearchable things you do not know. (Jeremiah 33:3)

When my child has a difficult decision to make, I pray they will call to You and ask for guidance. Teach my child great and unsearchable things that they could never learn on their own. Give them insight and wisdom beyond human explanation and man's comprehension.

The Shoulders: Burdens and Worries

> Ask and it will be given to you; seek and you will find; knock and the door will be opened to you. For everyone

who asks receives; the one who seeks finds; and to the one who knocks, the door will be opened. (Matthew 7:7–8)

Whatever my child needs today, I pray they will ask for Your help and knock on the door of Your supply closet rather than depending on their own ability alone. Thank You for the promise that everyone who asks receives, everyone who seeks finds, and to everyone who knocks, the door will be opened.

The Heart: Who and What My Child Loves

I have hidden your word in my heart that I might not sin against you. (Psalm 119:11)

I pray my child will hide Your word in their heart that they might not sin against You. May they keep Your word as a *treasure* to be protected and a plumb line to be practiced.

The Back: Physical and Spiritual Protection

Be strong and courageous. Do not be afraid or terrified because of them, for the LORD your God goes with you; he will never leave you nor forsake you. (Deuteronomy 31:6)

I pray my child will be strong and courageous knowing You go with us no matter where we go. Help them remember You will never leave or abandon them ... no matter what.

The Arms: Health and Strength

> Be strong in the Lord [draw your strength from Him and
> be empowered through your union with Him] and in the
> power of His [boundless] might. (Ephesians 6:10 AMP)

I pray my child will be strong in the Lord, drawing strength from Your mighty power. May they be empowered by Your Spirit to conquer giants, move mountains, and experience victory in the physical and spiritual realms.

The Hands: Gifts and Talents

> To these four young men God gave knowledge and
> understanding of all kinds of literature and learning.
> (Daniel 1:17a)

God, I pray You will give my child knowledge and understanding in schoolwork. Help them comprehend the concepts and apply the principles.

The Ring Finger: Future Spouse

> But you, be strong and do not lose courage, for there is a
> reward for your work. (2 Chronicles 15:7 NASB)

Lord, I pray my child's future spouse will grow up to be a person who does not give up easily—a person who does not give up when circumstances get rough or give in when resisting temptation gets tough. I ask You to equip, energize, and encourage this individual with the power of the Holy Spirit, and reward my child's future spouse in such a way that they know it comes from You.

The Side: Influential Relationships

> The righteous choose their friends carefully, but the way of the wicked leads them astray. (Proverbs 12:26)

I pray my child will be cautious about whom they choose as close friends. While we are called to be salt and light in the world and to befriend the lost as Jesus did, bring my child godly companions with whom they can form strong bonds—friends who will influence them to follow You more closely, love You more deeply, and listen to You more carefully.

Sexuality: Sexual Purity and Identity

> God blesses those who patiently endure testing and temptation. Afterward they will receive the crown of life that God has promised to those who love him. (James 1:12 NLT)

I pray You will give my child the courage and conviction to endure sexual testing and temptation. When they pass with flying colors, may they sense Your pleasure.

The Legs: Stand for Godly Principles

> My child, if sinners entice you, turn your back on them! (Proverbs 1:10 NLT)

If someone tries to entice my child to sin—engaging in activities that are immoral or looking at images that are sinful—I pray they will not give in but walk away. Give them the courage, confidence, and conviction to stand firm in what is right and walk away from what is wrong.

The Knees: Relationship with God

> Submit yourselves, then, to God. Resist the devil, and he will flee from you. Come near to God and he will come near to you. Wash your hands, you sinners, and purify your hearts, you double-minded. (James 4:7–8)

I pray my child will submit to Your authority rather than follow the world's majority. Give them the power to resist the devil in the name of Jesus. Help them to stay on course with the flow of truth.

The Feet: The Path My Child Takes

> Since we are surrounded by such a great cloud of witnesses, let us throw off everything that hinders and the sin that so easily entangles. And let us run with perseverance the race marked out for us, fixing our eyes on Jesus, the pioneer and perfecter of faith. (Hebrews 12:1–2a)

Finally, I pray my child will learn how to throw off everything that hinders them from running the great race of life well. May they strip off any sin that would tangle up their feet or slow down the pace. Give my child the stamina to run with perseverance the race You have marked out for them and not worry about the race You have marked out for someone else. Keep their eyes fixed on the goal of becoming more like Christ every day, and keep their feet on the right path to do so. I pray all this in Jesus' name, amen.

Day 22

The Mind: What My Child Thinks About

> Let the word of Christ dwell in you richly. (Colossians 3:16a ESV)

Dear Lord, I pray the word of Christ will dwell, take up residence, and feel completely at home in my child's mind—permeating every part of their being.

The Eyes: What My Child Looks At

> Everything in the world—the lust of the flesh, the lust of the eyes, and the pride of life—comes not from the Father but from the world. (1 John 2:16)

God, we know the lust of the eyes was the first step of the original sin. Eve saw, she wanted, and she took. I pray my child will have the willpower and strong resolve to resist the progression of sin by turning their eyes away from any temptation immediately.

The Ears: Who and What My Child Listens To

> With persuasive words she led him astray; she seduced him with her smooth talk. (Proverbs 7:21)

I pray my child will not listen to anyone who tries to lead them astray. Help them turn away from temptation and turn toward conviction.

The Mouth: Words My Child Speaks

> Do not lie to each other, since you have taken off your old self with its practices. (Colossians 3:9)

I pray my child will speak only what is truthful, no matter how difficult it may be or how enticing a tweak to the truth may seem.

The Neck: Decisions That Turn My Child's Head

> This is what the LORD says—your Redeemer, the Holy One of Israel: "I am the LORD your God, who teaches you what is best for you, who directs you in the way you should go." (Isaiah 48:17)

Lord, I ask You to teach my child what is best and direct them in the way they should go. I pray my child will not make decisions based on what peers and the popular crowd are doing but on what they know is right. Lead them to turn away from potentially harmful decisions and toward assuredly helpful choices.

The Shoulders: Burdens and Worries

> [Jesus said,] Come to me, all you who are weary and burdened, and I will give you rest. Take my yoke upon you and learn from me, for I am gentle and humble in heart, and you will find rest for your souls. For my yoke is easy and my burden is light. (Matthew 11:28–30)

Through prayer,
the enemy's plans
are intercepted;
the principalities
and authorities are
defeated. Through
prayer, the power
and provision of
God flow into the
lives of His people.

Jesus, when my child feels overburdened with the cares of this world, I pray they will come to You and rest in You. I pray they will take off the yoke of self-sufficiency and put on the yoke of Your all-sufficiency. I pray they will learn how to throw off the illusion that we must make life work in our own strength and, instead, embrace the truth that when we are weak, then You are strong.

The Heart: Who and What My Child Loves

> The heart is deceitful above all things and beyond cure. (Jeremiah 17:9a ESV)

While the world says, "Follow your heart; do what feels right," Your Word tells us the heart cannot be trusted; it is deceitful above all things. I pray my child will not rely on feelings but will sift every decision through the sieve of faith.

The Back: Physical and Spiritual Protection

> Show me the wonders of your great love, you who save by your right hand those who take refuge in you from their foes. Keep me as the apple of your eye; hide me in the shadow of your wings. (Psalm 17:7–8)

Almighty God, I pray You will show my child the wonders of Your great love as You save and protect them by Your right hand. Protect them from anyone or anything purposed to do them harm. Thank You, Lord, for keeping them as the apple of Your eye and hiding them in the shadow of Your wings.

The Arms: Health and Strength

> We also pray that you will be strengthened with all his glorious power so you will have all the endurance and patience you need. (Colossians 1:11a NLT)

I pray my child will be strengthened with all Your glorious power so they will have all the endurance and patience they need. Give them the stamina and fortitude to complete every task You have called them to do.

The Hands: Gifts and Talents

> Moses said to the people of Israel, "See, the LORD has called by name Bezalel the son of Uri, son of Hur, of the tribe of Judah; and he has filled him with the Spirit of God, with skill, with intelligence, with knowledge, and with all craftsmanship, to devise artistic designs, to work in gold and silver and bronze, in cutting stones for setting, and in carving wood, for work in every skilled craft. (Exodus 35:30–33 ESV)

Just as You empowered and equipped Bezalel to do work You had called him to do, please empower and equip my child to do the work You have called them to do.

The Ring Finger: Future Spouse

> Seek the Kingdom of God above all else, and live righteously, and he will give you everything you need. (Matthew 6:33 NLT)

Lord, there is so much pressure on young people today regarding who they should become and what they should do in life. I pray my child's future spouse will not get so caught up in trying to measure up to the world's standards of success that they end up neglecting a close relationship with You. I pray they will seek You above all else and rest assured that You will provide everything they need in life.

The Side: Influential Relationships

> Bear with each other and forgive one another if any of
> you has a grievance against someone. Forgive as the Lord
> forgave you. (Colossians 3:13)

Help my child be patient with others and forgive any grievances they may have. I pray they will not hold a grudge or plan revenge but release the offenses and let You take care of the rest.

Sexuality: Sexual Purity and Identity

> Every good and perfect gift is from above, coming down
> from the Father of the heavenly lights, who does not
> change like shifting shadows. (James 1:17)

I pray my child will understand that sex is not an evil to be avoided but a gift from God to be enjoyed and opened at just the right time.

The Legs: Stand for Godly Principles

> Our struggle is not against flesh and blood, but against
> the rulers, against the authorities, against the powers of
> this dark world and against the spiritual forces of evil in

the heavenly realms. Therefore put on the full armor of God, so that when the day of evil comes, you may be able to stand your ground, and after you have done everything, to stand. (Ephesians 6:12–13)

Father God, I know my child may not understand what goes on in the spiritual realm; however, I pray they will rest assured, knowing there is nothing to fear. Satan is a defeated foe. And even though there are still evil forces at work in the world today, greater is Jesus, who is in my child, than the evil that is in the world. Help my child understand the purpose of each piece of the armor of God and how to use it. When the devil tries to attack my child, help them to do everything to stand strong and not give an inch.

The Knees: Relationship with God

The Pharisee stood by himself and prayed: "God, I thank you that I am not like other people—robbers, evildoers, adulterers—or even like this tax collector. I fast twice a week and give a tenth of all I get." But the tax collector stood at a distance. He would not even look up to heaven, but beat his breast and said, "God, have mercy on me, a sinner." (Luke 18:11–13)

I pray my child will never boast like the Pharisee, who thought he was better than everybody else because he followed the rules, but will be humble like the tax collector, who sought Your mercy, grace, and forgiveness. Keep my child from becoming puffed up and prideful so that they will not need to be humbled by You.

The Feet: The Path My Child Takes

> Walk by the Spirit, and you will not gratify the desires of
> the flesh. (Galatians 5:16)

Finally, I pray my child will not walk according to the flesh, attempting to get their God-given needs met apart from Christ, but that they will walk according to the Spirit, being led by, controlled by, and yielded to the Holy Spirit's influence. I pray all this in Jesus' name, amen.

Day 23

The Mind: What My Child Thinks About

For God has not given us a spirit of fear, but of power and of love and of a sound mind. (2 Timothy 1:7 NKJV)

Dear Lord, I pray You will give my child a sound mind today. I pray they will have clear, concise, and controlled thinking. I pray against any spirit of confusion that would attempt to cloud their thinking or jumble their thoughts.

The Eyes: What My Child Looks At

The temptations in your life are no different from what others experience. And God is faithful. He will not allow the temptation to be more than you can stand. When you are tempted, he will show you a way out so that you can endure. (1 Corinthians 10:13 NLT)

Lord, thank You for not allowing my child to be tempted beyond what they are able to resist but always providing a way of escape. Help my child see the way of escape and take it.

The Ears: Who and What My Child Listens To

> Listen to my instruction and be wise; do not disregard it. Blessed are those who listen to me, watching daily at my doors, waiting at my doorway. For those who find me find life and receive favor from the LORD. (Proverbs 8:33–35)

I pray my child will listen to wise instruction and be wise—that they will not disregard wise counsel from parents, peers, and those in authority but will pay attention to and take stock in discerning words.

The Mouth: Words My Child Speaks

> The words of the reckless pierce like swords, but the tongue of the wise brings healing. (Proverbs 12:18)

I pray my child will speak words that heal and not hurt, bring peace and not pain, build others up and not tear others down. I pray my child will not speak recklessly without thinking but weigh their words carefully before they escape their lips.

The Neck: Decisions That Turn My Child's Head

> David inquired of the LORD, and he answered. (2 Samuel 5:23a)

When faced with a tough decision today, I pray my child will stop and pray before moving forward. Thank You for answering when they call to You.

The Shoulders: Burdens and Worries

Do not fear, for I am with you; do not be dismayed, for I am your God. I will strengthen you and help you; I will uphold you with my righteous right hand.... For I am the LORD, your God who takes hold of your right hand and says to you, Do not fear; I will help you. (Isaiah 41:10, 13)

Lord, I pray my child will not fear the future but remember that You have everything under control. Assure them that You can handle every difficulty—that nothing is too hard for You. Strengthen and uphold them, for You are the Lord God, who takes hold of our right hand.

The Heart: Who and What My Child Loves

Hope deferred makes the heart sick, but a longing fulfilled is a tree of life. (Proverbs 13:12)

Protect my child from losing hope and becoming heartsick. Align their longings with Your desires. May my child experience the joy that follows a longing fulfilled.

The Back: Physical and Spiritual Protection

The LORD is my rock, my fortress and my deliverer; my God is my rock, in whom I take refuge, my shield and the horn of my salvation, my stronghold. (Psalm 18:2)

Thank You, Lord, for being my child's Rock, Fortress, and Deliverer in whom they can take refuge. I pray that just as an animal's horn is a symbol of strength and a means of protection, You will be the horn of my child's salvation—their strength, protection, and stronghold of safety.

The Arms: Health and Strength

> You will receive power when the Holy Spirit comes on you. (Acts 1:8a)

Father, thank You for the promised Holy Spirit who indwells all believers. I pray my child will be filled with and empowered by the Holy Spirit. Deliver them from the tendency to depend on their own strength, and prompt them to access the power available to every child of God.

The Hands: Gifts and Talents

> From the fruit of their lips people are filled with good things, and the work of their hands brings them reward. (Proverbs 12:14)

I pray my child will see good things come from the work of their hands. Let them reap the fruit of honest labor. May they feel a sense of accomplishment from a job well done.

The Ring Finger: Future Spouse

> Let her be the one the LORD has chosen for my master's son. (Genesis 24:44b)

Father, I don't get to choose my child's spouse as Abraham's servant got to choose the wife for Isaac—but You do! I wouldn't want to do the choosing because I'd most likely make a terrible mess. You know exactly what my child needs in a spouse and, likewise, You know exactly what my child's future spouse needs in a marriage partner. I pray You will bring them together at just the right moment, assuring them without a shadow of a doubt that You have blessed this union.

The Side: Influential Relationships

> Do nothing out of selfish ambition or vain conceit. Rather, in humility value others above yourselves, not looking to your own interests but each of you to the interests of others. (Philippians 2:3–4)

I pray my child would do nothing out of selfish ambition or vain conceit but in humility value others' needs above their own. Keep my child from simply looking out for their own interests, and help them to also demonstrate genuine concern for others—seeking ways to help them succeed and fulfill their dreams.

Sexuality: Sexual Purity and Identity

> When tempted, no one should say, "God is tempting me." For God cannot be tempted by evil, nor does he tempt anyone; but each person is tempted when they are dragged away by their own evil desire and enticed. Then, after desire has conceived, it gives birth to sin; and sin, when it is full-grown, gives birth to death. (James 1:13–15)

I pray my child will never blame You when they fall into temptation, saying, "God made me this way." Let my child see that there is always a choice to give in to desire or to walk away. When temptation knocks at the door, I pray they will not open it or even look through the peephole to catch a quick glimpse.

The Legs: Stand for Godly Principles

> Peter and John replied, "Which is right in God's eyes: to listen to you, or to him? You be the judges! As for us, we cannot help speaking about what we have seen and heard." (Acts 4:19–20)

I know that if there is anything that can cause a child to question beliefs, it's peer pressure and the desire to fit in. I pray my child will resist the urge to conform to what is posted by peers on social media or played out in ungodly behavior. Give them the courage to stand for truth in the face of rejection, exclusion, or humiliation.

The Knees: Relationship with God

> A time is coming and has now come when the true worshipers will worship the Father in the Spirit and in truth, for they are the kind of worshipers the Father seeks. God is spirit, and his worshipers must worship in the Spirit and in truth. (John 4:23–24)

Father God, even though we attend church and practice spiritual disciplines in our home, I pray my child will never think mere religion or the traditions of men will get them into heaven. Show my child what it means to worship in the Spirit and in truth. I pray they will have a sweet, intimate relationship with You.

The Feet: The Path My Child Takes

> Whether you turn to the right or to the left, your ears will hear a voice behind you, saying, "This is the way; walk in it." (Isaiah 30:21)

Finally, Lord, wherever my child goes today, make them spiritually sensitive to Your voice saying, "This is the way; walk in it." Guide them to faithfully follow Your nudges and not be distracted by the world's bells and whistles. May Your Word be their road map and Your Holy Spirit their guide. I pray all this in Jesus' name, amen.

Day 24

The Mind: What My Child Thinks About

> Holy brothers and sisters, who share in the heavenly call-
> ing, fix your thoughts on Jesus, whom we acknowledge as
> our apostle and high priest. (Hebrews 3:1)

Dear Lord, I pray my child will fix their thoughts on Jesus today. I pray they will keep Jesus as the centerpiece of everything they believe and think. Even though the world, the flesh, and the devil will bombard them with distractions on every side, I pray my child will filter all thoughts through the sieve of truth.

The Eyes: What My Child Looks At

> We fix our eyes not on what is seen, but on what is unseen,
> since what is seen is temporary, but what is unseen is eter-
> nal. (2 Corinthians 4:18)

I pray my child won't fix their eyes only on what is seen and temporary but on what is unseen and eternal. May they not be focused on people, possessions, or position but on godly purposes, principles, and the promise of heaven.

The Ears: Who and What My Child Listens To

> The way of fools seems right to them, but the wise listen to advice. (Proverbs 12:15)

I pray my child will not make decisions based on their own self-centered desires but will instead listen to godly advice.

The Mouth: Words My Child Speaks

> Let your conversation be always full of grace, seasoned with salt, so that you may know how to answer everyone. (Colossians 4:6)

I pray my child's words will be full of grace and seasoned with salt so that they may know how to give everyone the best answer possible.

The Neck: Decisions That Turn My Child's Head

> I will walk about in freedom, for I have sought out your precepts. (Psalm 119:45)

I pray my child will seek out Your precepts—that they will frame choices in the context of Your truth. Even though they may not know a lot of Scripture at this point in life, I pray the Holy Spirit will lead them to make the best decisions possible.

The Shoulders: Burdens and Worries

> Consider how the wild flowers grow. They do not labor or spin. Yet I tell you, not even Solomon in all his splendor was dressed like one of these. If that is how God clothes

the grass of the field, which is here today, and tomorrow is thrown into the fire, how much more will he clothe you—you of little faith! (Luke 12:27–28)

Help my child to do their best and then leave the outcome to You. Remind them of how You take care of the lilies of the field, and help them trust that You will take care them as well.

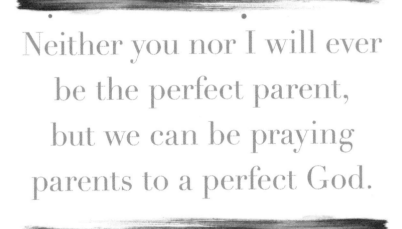

Neither you nor I will ever be the perfect parent, but we can be praying parents to a perfect God.

The Heart: Who and What My Child Loves

I say to you, love your enemies. Pray for those who hurt you. (Matthew 5:44 NCV)

Lord, rather than becoming bitter and resentful toward those who have hurt their feelings, may my child learn with Your help to pray for them instead. I know that's difficult to do, but I believe that You are the God who helps us to do the hard things.

The Back: Physical and Spiritual Protection

> You are my hiding place; you protect me from trouble.
> You surround me with songs of victory. (Psalm 32:7 NLT)

Father, be my child's hiding place. When they are afraid, may You be the place they run to for cover. Protect them from trouble, and surround them with songs of victory.

The Arms: Health and Strength

> The Sovereign LORD is my strength! He makes me
> as surefooted as a deer, able to tread upon the heights.
> (Habakkuk 3:19 NLT)

I pray my child will know that You, our Sovereign Lord, are our strength. Help them to remember that You make their arms strong for any battle and their legs steadfast for every journey. May they tread surefooted on the heights of every difficult circumstance and the depths of every craggy crisis.

The Hands: Gifts and Talents

> Strengthen the feeble hands, steady the knees that give
> way. (Isaiah 35:3)

When my child feels inferior, insecure, or inadequate because of school-work or teamwork, I ask You to strengthen their feeble hands and steady their weak knees. Give them the confidence, security, and courage to work with the steadfast hands of someone who is confident in the abilities and talents You have given them.

The Ring Finger: Future Spouse

> See what great love the Father has lavished on us, that we should be called children of God! And that is what we are! (1 John 3:1a)

I pray my child's future spouse will know that they are a dearly loved child of God, created in His image for a predetermined purpose. I pray against any feelings of inferiority, insecurity, and inadequacy that could hold my child's future spouse hostage to a life that is less than what You have planned.

The Side: Influential Relationships

> As God's chosen people, holy and dearly loved, clothe yourselves with compassion, kindness, humility, gentleness and patience. Bear with each other and forgive one another if any of you has a grievance against someone. Forgive as the Lord forgave you. And over all these virtues put on love, which binds them all together in perfect unity. (Colossians 3:12–14)

Dear Lord, thank You for choosing my child to be Yours—holy and dearly loved. I pray they will be clothed in compassion, kindness, gentleness, and patience. Help my child bear with the quirks of others who rub them the wrong way and forgive the offenses that may cause pain.

Most of all, I pray they will put on and wear love as the basic, all-purpose garment, never leaving home without it.

Sexuality: Sexual Purity and Identity

> Because we belong to the day, we must live decent lives for all to see. Don't participate in the darkness of wild parties and drunkenness, or in sexual promiscuity and immoral living, or in quarreling and jealousy. Instead, clothe yourself with the presence of the Lord Jesus Christ. And don't let yourself think about ways to indulge your evil desires. (Romans 13:13–14 NLT)

I pray my child will behave decently and honorably for all to see. Keep them from even thinking about or participating in any immoral sexual behavior—promiscuity or immoral living. Take away any evil cravings and replace them with godly desires.

The Legs: Stand for Godly Principles

> Brothers and sisters, I want to remind you of the gospel I preached to you, which you received and on which you have taken your stand. (1 Corinthians 15:1)

Lord, I pray my child will be a sponge that soaks up the Word all the days of their life. As they grow, mature, and eventually leave our home, I pray they will continue to take a stand for the truth and *never* waver in this morally ambiguous world that constantly changes what is right or wrong, good or bad, true or false.

The Knees: Relationship with God

> Very early in the morning, while it was still dark, Jesus got up, left the house and went off to a solitary place, where he prayed. (Mark 1:35)

I pray my child will grow into a person who is committed to prayer. I pray that prayer will not be something they consider an obligation that must be done but a privilege that can be done. Oh, Lord, make my child a person of prayer.

The Feet: The Path My Child Takes

> The LORD says, "I will guide you along the best pathway for your life. I will advise you and watch over you."
> (Psalm 32:8 NLT)

Finally, gracious Lord, please guide my child along the best path to follow. Advise them and watch over their every step along the way. I pray all this in Jesus' name, amen.

Day 25

The Mind: What My Child Thinks About

> As he thinks within himself, so he is. (Proverbs 23:7a NASB)

Lord, the Bible tells us that what we think about is who we become. I pray my child will remember and ruminate on the truth that they are specifically chosen, uniquely fashioned, and dearly loved by You so that they will live experientially what is already true spiritually.

The Eyes: What My Child Looks At

> Holy, holy, holy is the LORD Almighty; the whole earth is full of his glory. (Isaiah 6:3b)

I pray my child will see Your glory in all creation—in the small and large things of this world, the sunrise and the sunset, the minutiae of an insect and the grandness of the night sky.

The Ears: Who and What My Child Listens To

> Without consultation, plans are frustrated, but with many counselors they succeed. (Proverbs 15:22 NASB)

I pray my child will listen to wise counsel. Help them be able to discern the difference between advice that is wise, godly, and astute and that which is unwise, ungodly, and careless.

The Mouth: Words My Child Speaks

> Everyone should be quick to listen, slow to speak and slow to become angry. (James 1:19b)

I pray my child will be quick to listen, slow to speak, and slow to become angry. I pray they will not speak without listening first.

The Neck: Decisions That Turn My Child's Head

> Paul and his companions traveled throughout the region of Phrygia and Galatia, having been kept by the Holy Spirit from preaching the word in the province of Asia. When they came to the border of Mysia, they tried to enter Bithynia, but the Spirit of Jesus would not allow them to. (Acts 16:6–7)

What an exciting and encouraging Scripture! As my child makes decisions about where to go and what to do, increase their sensitivity to the Holy Spirit, especially when the Spirit is saying "Go," "Wait," or "Stay."

The Shoulders: Burdens and Worries

> Do not set your heart on what you will eat or drink; do not worry about it. For the pagan world runs after all such things, and your Father knows that you need them. But

seek his kingdom, and these things will be given to you as
well. (Luke 12:29–31)

How easily we let the hunger of our soul rumble with our culture's cravings. Rather than craving what will never satisfy their deepest longings,
may my child trust that You know exactly what they need. May their
relationship with You be their number-one priority throughout life. I
pray they will seek You and Your kingdom first and foremost throughout
life, knowing everything else will fall into place.

The Heart: Who and What My Child Loves

If I had cherished sin in my heart, the Lord would not
have listened; but God has surely listened and has heard
my prayer. (Psalm 66:18–19)

I pray my child will not cherish or hold on to any sin in their heart.
Convict them to confess sin quickly and repent from sin completely.

The Back: Physical and Spiritual Protection

God is our refuge and strength, an ever-present help in
trouble. Therefore we will not fear, though the earth
give way and the mountains fall into the heart of the
sea, though its waters roar and foam and the mountains
quake with their surging. (Psalm 46:1–3)

God, thank You for being my child's refuge and strength, an ever-present
help in trouble. No matter what happens in their life today, even if the

whole world seems to be falling apart, I pray they will not be afraid but will be confident that You will keep them safe and secure.

The Arms: Health and Strength

> God will strengthen you with his own great power so that you will not give up when troubles come, but you will be patient. (Colossians 1:11 NCV)

I pray my child will be strengthened with Your own great power so that they will not give up when troubles come but will be patient, persistent, and power-filled to see it through.

The Hands: Gifts and Talents

> Do everything without grumbling or arguing, so that you may become blameless and pure, "children of God without fault in a warped and crooked generation." Then you will shine among them like stars in the sky. (Philippians 2:14–15)

Help my child tackle the tasks of this day without grumbling, arguing, or complaining. May their positive attitude shine as a bright light in a dark world.

The Ring Finger: Future Spouse

> I pray that the eyes of your heart may be enlightened in order that you may know the hope to which he has called you, the riches of his glorious inheritance in his

holy people, and his incomparably great power for us who believe. (Ephesians 1:18–19a)

Lord, I pray You will open the eyes of my child's future spouse's heart so that they can know the hope to which You have called them and the great riches that are waiting for them in heaven. May my child's future spouse discover the incomparably great power of the Spirit that is in every believer. May they mature and grow in that understanding through the years.

The Side: Influential Relationships

> Make every effort to live in peace with everyone. (Hebrews 12:14a)

I pray my child will make every effort to live in peace in *every* relationship. I pray they will not harbor grudges but hand out grace.

Sexuality: Sexual Purity and Identity

> But among you there must not be even a hint of sexual immorality, or of any kind of impurity, or of greed, because these are improper for God's holy people. (Ephesians 5:3)

I pray there will not be even a hint of sexual immorality or of any kind of impurity in my child's thoughts or actions. Help them remember that You have set believers apart to live differently than the way the rest of the world lives.

The Legs: Stand for Godly Principles

It is by faith you stand firm. (2 Corinthians 1:24b)

Father, I know my child cannot depend on *my* faith in You but must make it their own. I pray they will stand firm in personal convictions, maturing to be a person of God who follows You all the days of their life.

The Knees: Relationship with God

Devote yourselves to prayer with an alert mind and a thankful heart. (Colossians 4:2 NLT)

I pray my child will learn how to pray with an alert mind and a thankful heart.

The Feet: The Path My Child Takes

The LORD makes firm the steps of the one who delights in him; though he may stumble, he will not fall, for the LORD upholds him with his hand. (Psalm 37:23–24)

Lastly, I pray my child will walk in a way that delights You so that You will make their steps firm. If they stumble along the way, catch my child with Your hand, Lord, and keep them from falling. I pray all this in Jesus' name, amen.

Day 26

The Mind: What My Child Thinks About

If any of you lacks wisdom, you should ask God, who gives generously to all without finding fault, and it will be given to you. But when you ask, you must believe and not doubt, because the one who doubts is like a wave of the sea, blown and tossed by the wind. That person should not expect to receive anything from the Lord. Such a person is double-minded and unstable in all they do. (James 1:5–8)

Father, I pray my child will not be double-minded in any way. I pray their mind will not be tossed about like a toy boat between belief and doubt, trust and worry, peace and anxiety, the world's ideas and biblical truth. Instead, I pray their faith will be like a steady ship on the quiet waters of belief.

The Eyes: What My Child Looks At

Be alert and of sober mind. Your enemy the devil prowls around like a roaring lion looking for someone to devour. (1 Peter 5:8)

I pray my child will pay attention to what they look at today. I pray they will be alert to the devil's tactics to entice them with visually tempting images and that they will show restraint and self-control by clicking delete or turning away, thus defeating the devil's schemes.

The Ears: Who and What My Child Listens To

> With their words, the godless destroy their friends, but knowledge will rescue the righteous. (Proverbs 11:9 NLT)

I pray my child will not listen to or internalize a friend's hurtful words but will pay close attention to and personalize positive words. I pray they will disregard words that are meant to tear down and embrace words that are meant to build up.

The Mouth: Words My Child Speaks

> The LORD detests lying lips, but he delights in people who are trustworthy. (Proverbs 12:22)

I pray my child will always tell the truth and be worthy of other people's trust.

The Neck: Decisions That Turn My Child's Head

> Do not be foolish, but understand what the Lord's will is. (Ephesians 5:17)

I pray my child will not be foolish or careless in deciding what to do, say, or be but will understand what You would have them do, say, or be.

Even if their decision is opposite of what friends are doing, give them the courage to say yes and no with confidence.

The Shoulders: Burdens and Worries

> [Jesus said,] Peace I leave with you; my peace I give you.
> I do not give to you as the world gives. Do not let your
> hearts be troubled and do not be afraid. (John 14:27)

When everyone else is in a panic because of world events, I pray my child will have a peace that only You can give. I pray their heart will not be troubled or afraid because of political turmoil or world affairs but will instead be at rest knowing You are in control.

The Heart: Who and What My Child Loves

> A cheerful heart is good medicine, but a crushed spirit
> dries up the bones. (Proverbs 17:22)

I pray my child will have a cheerful heart—not being prone to discouragement, depression, dejection, or despair but having so much joy that they will laugh easily and smile readily. I pray they will have a cheerful heart and a positive attitude, which is like good medicine.

The Back: Physical and Spiritual Protection

> As the mountains surround Jerusalem, so the LORD sur-
> rounds his people both now and forevermore. (Psalm 125:2)

Lord, I ask You to surround my child like the protective mountain range that surrounds Jerusalem, both now and forevermore.

The Arms: Health and Strength

> We have this treasure in jars of clay to show that this
> all-surpassing power is from God and not from us.
> (2 Corinthians 4:7)

Thank You, Lord, that my child, this wonderful jar of clay fashioned by Your hand, contains treasure placed specifically in them. I pray my child will be a container and conduit of Your power that flows in and through them.

The Hands: Gifts and Talents

> I can do everything through Christ, who gives me
> strength. (Philippians 4:13 NLT)

Thank You for the gifts and talents You have given my child. I know at some point they will become frustrated while developing those abilities. When that happens, help them remember that they can do all things through Christ's power that works in and through us.

The Ring Finger: Future Spouse

> The fruit of the Spirit is love, joy, peace, forbearance,
> kindness, goodness, faithfulness, gentleness and self-
> control. (Galatians 5:22–23a)

I pray my child's future spouse will develop the fruits of the Spirit: love, joy, peace, patience, kindness, goodness, faithfulness, gentleness, and self-control. Bless them with people to show what those qualities look and act like. Let them experience the difference between deep-seated joy and temporary happiness. May my child's future spouse find the source of true peace in a world of confusion and counterfeits. Let them see the difference between infatuation and deep-seated love.

The Side: Influential Relationships

> Encourage one another and build each other up, just as in fact you are doing. (1 Thessalonians 5:11)

Loving Lord, I pray my child will be an encourager in every relationship. Show them how to build others up and not tear them down. Teach them how to fan the flames of enthusiasm and not quench the embers of excitement. And Lord, provide someone to do that for my child as well.

Sexuality: Sexual Purity and Identity

> You created my inmost being; you knit me together in my mother's womb. I praise you because I am fearfully and wonderfully made; your works are wonderful, I know that full well. (Psalm 139:13–14)

I pray my child will know they were created on purpose for a purpose— that You knit them together in a mother's womb. I pray they will know their gender was planned from the beginning of time. I pray they will never desire to be anything other than what You have created them to be.

The Legs: Stand for Godly Principles

> Epaphras … is always wrestling in prayer for you, that you may stand firm in all the will of God, mature and fully assured. (Colossians 4:12)

Just as Epaphras was always wrestling in prayer for the Colossians, I continue to wrestle in prayer for my child. I pray they may stand firm in Your will, growing more spiritually mature every day, confident and fully assured in everything You want them to do.

The Knees: Relationship with God

> Now when Daniel learned that the decree had been published, he went home to his upstairs room where the windows opened toward Jerusalem. Three times a day he got down on his knees and prayed, giving thanks to his God, just as he had done before. (Daniel 6:10)

Fill my child with the power of the Holy Spirit so they will not let any anyone or anything prevent them from worshipping You. May they be like young Daniel, who refused to hide his faith even though it was punishable by death. No matter what happens, may they bend the knee and pray, giving thanks to God.

The Feet: The Path My Child Takes

> Observe the commands of the LORD your God, walking in obedience to him and revering him. (Deuteronomy 8:6)

Finally, Lord, I pray my child will keep Your commandments, walk in obedience, and show reverent respect for You. I pray all this in Jesus' name, amen.

Day 27

The Mind: What My Child Thinks About

> Solid food is for the mature, who by constant use have trained
> themselves to distinguish good from evil. (Hebrews 5:14)

Almighty God, I pray that as my child matures, they will crave the solid
food of Your Word. I pray they will never be satisfied with spoon-feeding
by pastors and teachers but will take up fork and knife to dig in to the
meat of the Scriptures on their own.

The Eyes: What My Child Looks At

> Immediately, something like scales fell from Saul's' eyes,
> and he could see again. (Acts 9:18a)

Just as You removed the scales from Saul's eyes so he could see again, I
pray You will remove any scales from my child's eyes that would keep
them from seeing You and Your will.

The Ears: Who and What My Child Listens To

> You were running well; who hindered you from obeying
> the truth? (Galatians 5:7 NASB)

I pray my child will not listen to anyone or anything that would hinder them from obeying and believing the truth. I pray they won't allow man-made religious ideas to slip into their mind through the portal of their ears. Instead, may they line up every teaching, opinion, and point of view with the plumb line of the gospel.

The Mouth: Words My Child Speaks

> Telling lies about others is as harmful as hitting them with an ax, wounding them with a sword, or shooting them with a sharp arrow. (Proverbs 25:18 NLT)

I pray my child will not hurt anyone with the sword of lies, the ax of accusation, or the arrow of harmful or hurtful words.

The Neck: Decisions That Turn My Child's Head

> This is my prayer: that your love may abound more and more in knowledge and depth of insight, so that you may be able to discern what is best and may be pure and blameless for the day of Christ. (Philippians 1:9–10)

This is my prayer: that my child's love may abound more and more in knowledge and depth of insight so that they may be able to discern what is best and make the best decisions until You return or take us home.

The Shoulders: Burdens and Worries

> Nothing will be impossible with God. (Luke 1:37 ESV)

When my child feels hopeless or helpless, remind them of this truth: nothing is impossible with You. Remove worries and fears, and replace them with peace and trust. Assure them that nothing is too heavy for You to carry, too difficult for You to fix, too broken for You to mend.

The Heart: Who and What My Child Loves

> My heart, O God, is steadfast, my heart is steadfast; I will sing and make music. (Psalm 57:7)

I pray my child's heart will be steadfast and secure in who they are in Christ, what they have in Christ, and where they are in Christ. Remove any feelings of inferiority, insecurity, or inadequacy that would threaten to hold them back, and replace those feelings with a God-confidence that will move them forward. Put a song of praise in their heart today.

The Back: Physical and Spiritual Protection

> The weapons we fight with are not the weapons of the world. On the contrary, they have divine power to demolish strongholds. (2 Corinthians 10:4)

Thank You, Father, that we have divine power to demolish strongholds through prayer. I come against anyone or anything in the spiritual or physical realms that would seek to harm my child today. I hold up the shield of faith to block the fiery arrows and wield the sword of the Spirit, which is the Word of God.

The Arms: Health and Strength

> For this reason I kneel before the Father, from whom every family in heaven and on earth derives its name.

I pray that out of his glorious riches he may strengthen
you with power through his Spirit in your inner being,
so that Christ may dwell in your hearts through faith.
(Ephesians 3:14–17a)

Father, I kneel before You and pray that out of Your glorious riches You
will strengthen my child with power through the Holy Spirit in their
inner being so that Christ may dwell in them through faith. I pray they
will experience good health, a strong body, and a sound mind.

The Hands: Gifts and Talents

Who makes you different from anyone else? What do you
have that you did not receive? And if you did receive it, why
do you boast as though you did not? (1 Corinthians 4:7)

Help my child to remember that every intellectual and physical ability
they have is a gift from You. I pray they will thank You for the gift and
never think their accomplishments were by their own merits and abilities
alone.

The Ring Finger: Future Spouse

Do not be foolish, but understand what the Lord's will is.
(Ephesians 5:17)

I pray my child's future spouse will not be foolish or careless in deciding
what to do, say, or be but instead understand what Your will is. I pray
they will make good decisions throughout life, even if those decisions are
opposite of what those around them are doing.

The Side: Influential Relationships

> Two are better than one, because they have a good return
> for their labor: If either of them falls down, one can help
> the other up. But pity anyone who falls and has no one to
> help them up. (Ecclesiastes 4:9–10)

Lord, please give my child at least one godly friend who will encourage
them. Let this person be the type of friend who will not desert someone
when they fall but instead help them get back on their feet.

Sexuality: Sexual Purity and Identity

> Your hands made me and formed me; give me under-
> standing to learn your commands. (Psalm 119:73)

Father, I pray my child will always remember that Your hands made and
formed them—it wasn't happenstance or circumstance. I pray against
any gender confusion and cultural delusion that would cause them to
doubt who and what You have created them to be.

The Legs: Stand for Godly Principles

> Brothers and sisters, stand firm and hold fast to the teach-
> ings we passed on to you, whether by word of mouth or
> by letter. (2 Thessalonians 2:15)

I pray my child will defy the statistics of teenagers who leave the faith
once they leave the home. Instead, I pray that they will stand firm on
the teaching they learned as a child. Whether it came from parents,
peers, preachers, or pastors, I pray they will not falter in their faith,

waver in their walk, or allow anyone or anything to weaken their stance for truth.

The Knees: Relationship with God

> This is good, and pleases God our Savior, who wants all people to be saved and to come to a knowledge of the truth. (1 Timothy 2:3–4)

Thank You, God, that You want all people to be saved and come to a knowledge of the truth. I pray my child will come to faith, confessing with their mouth that Jesus is Lord and believing in their heart that You raised Him from the dead. I also pray they will continue to grow deeper in the knowledge of the truth.

The Feet: The Path My Child Takes

> He will not let your foot slip—he who watches over you will not slumber; indeed, he who watches over Israel will neither slumber nor sleep. (Psalm 121:3–4)

Finally, what a comfort to know that You never slumber; indeed, You who watch over my child will neither slumber nor sleep. I pray You will not let my child's foot slip—that they will not stumble on the rocks of temptation or fall into the ditches of sin. Open their eyes to detect the precisely positioned snares of the enemy intended to trip them up and bring them down. I pray all this in Jesus' name, amen.

Day 28

The Mind: What My Child Thinks About

My goal is that they may be encouraged in heart and united in love, so that they may have the full riches of complete understanding, in order that they may know the mystery of God, namely, Christ, in whom are hidden all the treasures of wisdom and knowledge. I tell you this so that no one may deceive you by fine-sounding arguments. (Colossians 2:2–4)

Father, my goal is the same as Paul's for the Colossians. I long for my child to be encouraged in heart and united in love so that they may have the full riches of complete understanding in their mind, in order that they may know the mystery of God, namely, Christ, in whom are hidden all the treasures of wisdom and knowledge. Then they will have a mind that is confident and at rest and focused on Christ, who causes everything else in life to make sense. I pray they will not be led offtrack by hollow or deceptive philosophies, false doctrines, or New Age religions.

The Eyes: What My Child Looks At

The LORD said to Samuel, "Do not consider his appearance or his height, for I have rejected him. The LORD does not look at the things people look at. People look at the outward appearance, but the LORD looks at the heart." (1 Samuel 16:7)

I pray my child will not make decisions about others by what they see on the outside but by what is in a person's heart on the inside.

The Ears: Who and What My Child Listens To

We are God's masterpiece. He has created us anew in Christ Jesus, so we can do the good things he planned for us long ago. (Ephesians 2:10 NLT)

I pray my child will not listen to anyone who says they are not good enough, strong enough, smart enough, or attractive enough. I pray they will always remember they are God's masterpiece, a uniquely fashioned work of art who is empowered by the Father, equipped by the Holy Spirit, and enveloped by Jesus Christ.

The Mouth: Words My Child Speaks

Likewise, the tongue is a small part of the body, but it makes great boasts. Consider what a great forest is set on fire by a small spark. (James 3:5)

I pray my child will not use contentious words to start a forest fire of trouble but calming ones to extinguish sparks before they spread.

The Neck: Decisions That Turn My Child's Head

> Do not be anxious about anything, but in every situation,
> by prayer and petition, with thanksgiving, present your
> requests to God. (Philippians 4:6)

I pray my child will not be anxious about the decisions they have to make but will pray about everything with thanksgiving, presenting requests to You. Thank You in advance for the answers that are sure to come.

The Shoulders: Burdens and Worries

> My God will meet all your needs according to the riches
> of his glory in Christ Jesus. (Philippians 4:19)

All-sufficient God, I know You will meet all my child's needs according to Your glorious riches in Christ Jesus. I pray they will learn to ask for Your help, for then You will surely give it.

The Heart: Who and What My Child Loves

> Blessed is the one who always trembles before God, but who-
> ever hardens their heart falls into trouble. (Proverbs 28:14)

Lord, give my child a malleable heart. May they always respect You, revere You, and submit to You. Keep their heart from becoming hardened through any form of disobedience or rebellion so that they won't fall into trouble.

The Back: Physical and Spiritual Protection

> Whoever dwells in the shelter of the Most High will rest
> in the shadow of the Almighty. I will say of the LORD,

"He is my refuge and my fortress, my God, in whom I trust." (Psalm 91:1–2)

I pray my child will choose to dwell in the shelter of Your protection and rest in the shadow of Your care. I pray they will trust that You are their safe place.

The people we choose to walk side by side with in relationship affects our choices, character, and conduct for good or bad.

The Arms: Health and Strength

Let all that I am praise the LORD; may I never forget the good things he does for me. He forgives all my sins and heals all my diseases. (Psalm 103:2–3 NLT)

Father, I praise You for being our Savior and Healer. I pray my child will experience good health. However, when sickness comes, as it surely will, I pray You will heal my child quickly and completely. Thank You for giving doctors the gifts and talents needed to help mend our bodies.

Lead us to the right physicians when necessary. Thank You for healing all our diseases.

The Hands: Gifts and Talents

> What he [the Holy One] opens no one can shut, and what
> he shuts no one can open. (Revelation 3:7b)

Lord, as my child develops the gifts and talents You have given, I pray You will open the right doors for them to walk through and close the wrong ones to keep them out. Keep them from trying to force doors open that You intend to remain shut. Give them the courage to walk through the door that You have flung open. Bless them with the discernment to know the difference.

The Ring Finger: Future Spouse

> Keep this Book of the Law always on your lips; meditate
> on it day and night, so that you may be careful to do
> everything written in it. Then you will be prosperous and
> successful. (Joshua 1:8)

I pray my child's future spouse will have a love for Your Word—that they will meditate on the Scriptures and saturate their soul with Your Word. May they allow the Bible to be the plumb line for every action so that they will be prosperous and successful.

The Side: Influential Relationships

> All of you, be like-minded, be sympathetic, love one
> another, be compassionate and humble. (1 Peter 3:8)

I pray my child will be like-minded with other Christian brothers and sisters—being sympathetic, compassionate, and humble. Give them many Christian friends who will be the same for them.

Sexuality: Sexual Purity and Identity

> How foolish can you be? He is the Potter, and he is certainly greater than you, the clay! Should the created thing say of the one who made it, "He didn't make me"? Does a jar ever say, "The potter who made me is stupid"? (Isaiah 29:16 NLT)

Prayer for a Son: Father, the world is so mixed up. How foolish can it be? May my son always know that the Potter, who formed him to be a male, was not stupid and did not make a mistake but made him a male on purpose for a purpose. I come against the world, the flesh, and the devil that would tell him otherwise.

Prayer for a Daughter: May my daughter always know that the Potter, who formed her to be a female, was not stupid and did not make a mistake but made her to be a female on purpose for a purpose. I come against the world, the flesh, and the devil, all of which would tell her otherwise.

The Legs: Stand for Godly Principles

> Remember that I have commanded you to be determined and confident! Do not be afraid or discouraged, for I, the LORD your God, am with you wherever you go. (Joshua 1:9 GNT)

Lord, I know how hard it is to stand up against the crowd and stand for the crown. I remember how difficult it was in my own life. I pray my child will be strong and courageous, that they will not be afraid or become discouraged when standing up means standing out. I pray they will remember that You will be with them wherever they go.

The Knees: Relationship with God

> Whom have I in heaven but you? I desire you more than anything on earth. (Psalm 73:25 NLT)

I pray my child will not love anyone or anything more than You. May You always have first place in their heart.

The Feet: The Path My Child Takes

> To him who is able to keep you from stumbling and to present you before his glorious presence without fault and with great joy—to the only God our Savior be glory, majesty, power and authority, through Jesus Christ our Lord, before all ages, now and forevermore! Amen. (Jude 1:24–25)

Finally, I praise You, Lord, because You can keep my child from stumbling or falling. I pray You will keep them standing on their feet without slipping or sliding into sin. I pray Jesus will present them before Your glorious presence without fault and with great joy. To the only God our Savior be glory, majesty, power, and authority, through Jesus Christ our Lord, before all ages, now and forevermore! I pray all this in Jesus' name, amen.

Day 29

The Mind: What My Child Thinks About

God is not a God of confusion but of peace. (1 Corinthians 14:33a ESV)

Father, I know that You are not a God of confusion. I pray my child's mind will not be confused by the current culture but will be clear on scriptural truth. Help them see the fallacies of moral relativism and human ideologies and cling to the certainties and consistencies of Your Word.

The Eyes: What My Child Looks At

I keep my eyes always on the LORD. With him at my right hand, I will not be shaken. (Psalm 16:8)

I pray my child will keep their eyes always on the Lord, knowing that with Jesus at their side, they will not be shaken.

The Ears: Who and What My Child Listens To

Come to me with your ears wide open. Listen, and you will find life. I will make an everlasting covenant with you. I will give you all the unfailing love I promised to David. (Isaiah 55:3 NLT)

I pray my child will come to You with ears wide open! I pray they will listen closely to Your life-giving words. Help them to understand that listening to You will lead to the best life possible—more than they could ever imagine or hope for.

The Mouth: Words My Child Speaks

Bless those who persecute you; bless and do not curse them. (Romans 12:14 ESV)

When someone says something bad about my child to my child, I pray they will surprise that person by saying something nice in return.

The Neck: Decisions That Turn My Child's Head

If you need wisdom, ask our generous God, and he will give it to you. He will not rebuke you for asking. (James 1:5 NLT)

When my child needs wisdom to make the right decision, I pray they will ask You for help. May they be sensitive to the Spirit's leading and courageous to follow through.

The Shoulders: Burdens and Worries

To him who is able to do immeasurably more than all we ask or imagine, according to his power that is at work within us, to him be glory in the church and in

Christ Jesus throughout all generations, for ever and ever! (Ephesians 3:20–21)

Lord, whatever pressures my child may face today and throughout life, help them remember that You are able to do immeasurably more than all they could ask or imagine. Prompt them to cling to the truth that You can accomplish more through a willing servant in one day than a self-sufficient person can accomplish in a lifetime.

The Heart: Who and What My Child Loves

Christ loved the church and gave himself up for her. (Ephesians 5:25b)

Lord, I pray my child will love church. I pray they will not begrudge going to church but look forward to gathering with Christians. Jesus loved the church so much that He gave Himself up for her. I pray my child will have the same passion and will always want to be an active member of a Bible-teaching body. I also pray they will make good friends at the church our family attends.

The Back: Physical and Spiritual Protection

Angels are only servants—spirits sent to care for people who will inherit salvation. (Hebrews 1:14 NLT)

Father, I pray You will surround my child with a host of angels today. May heavenly hosts watch over them, protecting them from physical harm and spiritual ambush.

The Arms: Health and Strength

> May the God of hope fill you with all joy and peace as you
> trust in him, so that you may overflow with hope by the
> power of the Holy Spirit. (Romans 15:13)

I pray You will fill my child with all joy and peace as they learn to trust
in You, so that they will overflow with hope by the power of the Holy
Spirit. Give them strength when they are weak, power when they are
powerless, courage when they are afraid.

The Hands: Gifts and Talents

> Each of you has your own gift from God; one has this
> gift, another has that. (1 Corinthians 7:7b)

Lord, thank You for giving my child gifts and talents. I pray they will
discover what those gifts are and use them to glorify You. I pray they
won't envy someone else's abilities but will be thankful for their own.

The Ring Finger: Future Spouse

> We are His workmanship, created in Christ Jesus for
> good works, which God prepared beforehand so that we
> would walk in them. (Ephesians 2:10 NASB)

I pray my child's future spouse will remember that each one of us is
Your masterpiece—Your work of art—that You created for a preordained
purpose and a plan. May my child's future spouse grow up knowing that
they are Your image-bearer with gifts and talents that You specifically
designed for them.

The Side: Influential Relationships

> Shadrach, Meshach and Abednego replied to him, "King
> Nebuchadnezzar, we do not need to defend ourselves
> before you in this matter. If we are thrown into the blaz-
> ing furnace, the God we serve is able to deliver us from it,
> and he will deliver us from Your Majesty's hand. But even
> if he does not, we want you to know, Your Majesty, that
> we will not serve your gods or worship the image of gold
> you have set up." (Daniel 3:16–18)

Just as these three young friends stood together against King Nebuchadnezzar and endured the fiery furnace, I pray my child will have
friends who will stand together with them to endure the fiery trials of
this life.

Sexuality: Sexual Purity and Identity

> [Jesus said] At the beginning of creation God "made
> them male and female." "For this reason a man will leave
> his father and mother and be united to his wife, and the
> two will become one flesh." So they are no longer two,
> but one flesh. Therefore what God has joined together, let
> no one separate. (Mark 10:6–9)

I pray my child will understand that You created humans to be male or
female—that You have not made any mistakes by giving the wrong body
parts to the wrong person.

The Legs: Stand for Godly Principles

> Stand up and bless the LORD your God from everlasting to everlasting. Blessed be your glorious name, which is exalted above all blessing and praise. (Nehemiah 9:5b ESV)

I pray my child will become a person who stands up and blesses You from everlasting to everlasting. I pray they will bless Your glorious name, which is exalted above all blessings and praise. I pray they will not place hope in earthly things that the world craves but see temporary trappings as potential shackles.

The Knees: Relationship with God

> Exalt the LORD our God! Bow low before his feet, for he is holy! (Psalm 99:5 NLT)

I pray my child will never forget that You are almighty God, who deserves all honor and glory forever. Give them a sense of awe that causes them to bow before You in adoration and exaltation.

The Feet: The Path My Child Takes

> Who are those who fear the LORD? He will show them the path they should choose. (Psalm 25:12 NLT)

Finally, Lord, I pray my child will honor and revere You as King of Kings and Lord of Lords. I pray You will show them the path they should choose and that they will take it. I pray all this in Jesus' name, amen.

Day 30

The Mind: What My Child Thinks About

My child, never forget the things I have taught you. Store my commands in your heart. If you do this, you will live many years, and your life will be satisfying. (Proverbs 3:1–2 NLT)

I pray my child will never forget the things I (and my husband) have taught them. May they store my instructions in their heart and mind so that they can have a long, satisfying life.

The Eyes: What My Child Looks At

Let us run with perseverance the race marked out for us, fixing our eyes on Jesus, the pioneer and perfecter of faith. (Hebrews 12:1b–2a)

Lord, I pray my child will run the race You have marked out for them, keeping their eyes on Jesus, the pioneer and perfecter of faith. I pray they will not be distracted by flashy enticements of the world but stay focused on the advancement of spiritual growth.

The Ears: Who and What My Child Listens To

> She [Martha] had a sister called Mary, who sat at the
> Lord's feet listening to what he said. (Luke 10:39)

Father, I pray my child will learn what it means to "sit at Jesus' feet" to listen to what He is saying. Open their spiritual ears to hear Your still, small voice. As they begin their own prayer journey, help them to not only talk to You but also hear from You.

The Mouth: Words My Child Speaks

> Do you see a man who is hasty in his words? There is
> more hope for a fool than for him. (Proverbs 29:20 ESV)

I pray my child will not be hasty and careless with words but weigh them carefully before they speak.

The Neck: Decisions That Turn My Child's Head

> Solid food is for those who are mature, who through
> training have the skill to recognize the difference between
> right and wrong. (Hebrews 5:14 NLT)

I pray my child will grow and become emotionally and spiritually mature—moving from merely drinking the pure milk of the Word to chewing on the solid food of deep spiritual truths. As they move toward adulthood, I pray they will learn how to discern between what is right and wrong, good and evil, better and best.

The Shoulders: Burdens and Worries

> Blessed is the one who trusts in the LORD, whose con-
> fidence is in him. They will be like a tree planted by the
> water that sends out its roots by the stream. It does not
> fear when heat comes; its leaves are always green. It has no
> worries in a year of drought and never fails to bear fruit.
> (Jeremiah 17:7–8)

I pray my child will not worry or fret about the future but confidently
trust in Your sovereign plan. I pray they will be like a tree planted by the
water that sends out its roots by the stream—that they will not worry
when difficult seasons come but continue to be productive.

The Heart: Who and What My Child Loves

> There is neither Jew nor Gentile, neither slave nor free,
> nor is there male and female, for you are all one in Christ
> Jesus. (Galatians 3:28)

Father, in our world today there are more divisions than ever before. I
pray my child will not have any racial, societal, intellectual, economic,
or gender prejudice but will see every person as someone created in the
image of God. Help them remember that You show no partiality but
gave Your Son as a sacrifice for all [John 3:16].

The Back: Physical and Spiritual Protection

> When you pass through the waters, I will be with you;
> and when you pass through the rivers, they will not sweep

over you. When you walk through the fire, you will not
be burned; the flames will not set you ablaze. (Isaiah 43:2)

When my child passes through rough waters of life and begins to feel
overwhelmed, set their feet on dry ground. When they walk through
fiery trials and feel as if everything is about to go up in flames, extinguish the blaze. No matter what trials come their way today, remind
them that You are there for protection and deliverance.

The Arms: Health and Strength

When we brought you the Good News, it was not only
with words but also with power, for the Holy Spirit
gave you full assurance that what we said was true.
(1 Thessalonians 1:5a NLT)

I pray my child will understand and believe that Scripture is not simply words on a page but the very power of God given to us. I pray the
power of the Holy Spirit will put steel in their convictions, bring fire
in their faith, and give them the strength to withstand any struggle.

The Hands: Gifts and Talents

The LORD your God has blessed you in all the work of
your hands. (Deuteronomy 2:7a)

Thank You for my child's gifts and talents. I pray You will bless all
the work of their hands.

The Ring Finger: Future Spouse

> As for me and my household, we will serve the LORD.
> (Joshua 24:15b)

As my child's future spouse grows into an adult, I pray they will have the conviction that no matter what, they will say with resolve, "As for me and my household, we will serve the Lord." I pray this for my child's future family and for generations yet to come.

> Relationships are the change agents God uses to sand away the rough edges of the flesh and shore up the weak places of the soul.

The Side: Influential Relationships

> Do not make friends with a hot-tempered person, do not
> associate with one easily angered, or you may learn their
> ways and get yourself ensnared. (Proverbs 22:24–25)

I pray my child will not make close friends with people who are hot-tempered or easily angered so that person's actions and reactions won't influence theirs.

Sexuality: Sexual Purity and Identity

> Dear brothers and sisters, I plead with you to give your bod-
> ies to God because of all he has done for you. Let them be a
> living and holy sacrifice—the kind he will find acceptable.
> This is truly the way to worship him. (Romans 12:1 NLT)

I pray my child will dedicate their body to God—that they will be a living and holy sacrifice—set apart for holy purposes. I pray they will not give in to sexual urges of youth but wait until marriage, when the gift of sex can be experienced with celebration and without shame.

The Legs: Stand for Godly Principles

> They will be called oaks of righteousness, a planting of
> the LORD for the display of his splendor. (Isaiah 61:3b)

I pray my child will grow to be an oak of righteousness, a planting of the Lord for the display of His splendor. I pray they will stand firmly planted in the soil of Your truth and watered by Your Spirit, not shaken by the winds of change or parched by the drought of uncertainty.

The Knees: Relationship with God

> He guides the humble in what is right and teaches them
> his way. (Psalm 25:9)

Lord, keep my child from being proud and making the mistake of thinking that life can be handled on their own. I pray they will instead bend the knee in humility before You. I ask that they will learn from You and live for You.

The Feet: The Path My Child Takes

> Now all glory to God, who is able to keep you from
> falling away and will bring you with great joy into his
> glorious presence without a single fault. All glory to him
> who alone is God, our Savior through Jesus Christ our
> Lord. All glory, majesty, power, and authority are his
> before all time, and in the present, and beyond all time!
> Amen. (Jude 1:24–25 NLT)

Finally, I praise You, Lord, because I know You are able to keep my child from falling away. I hold on to the promise that You will bring my child before You without a single fault! All glory to You alone, our God, our Savior through Jesus Christ our Lord. All glory, majesty, power, and authority are Yours before all time, and in the present, and beyond all time! I pray all this in Jesus' name, amen.

Appendix

There are some areas of a child's life that weigh on a parent's heart and callus the knees. I've added three specific struggles in the appendix for targeted prayer: prayers for the prodigal to return, prayers for the sick to be healed, and prayers for salvation for the not-yet decided. You'll find ten Scriptures and ten prayers for each of these areas. If your child fits into one of these categories, I encourage you to pray these ten prayers often. Remember: "The earnest prayer of a righteous person has great power and produces wonderful results" (James 5:16b NLT). "This is the confidence that we have toward him, that if we ask anything according to his will he hears us. And if we know that he hears us in whatever we ask, we know that we have the requests that we have asked of him" (1 John 5:14–15 ESV).

Prayer for Healing

I'll never forget the day when my four-year-old son was lying in a hospital bed, with nurses trying to get an IV into his tiny arm. He had been as limp as a rag doll with dehydration from the flu, but when the nurse tried to place the life-giving fluid in his vein, he fought with all he had.

"Help me, Mommy! Make them stop!" he cried. With tears streaming down my cheeks, I stood in the corner, assuring him, "They aren't trying to hurt you. They're going to make you all better." I don't know who cried the most—Steven, me, or the nurses.

A mother's heart aches to see her child suffering with any kind of sickness, be it a short-term ailment or a long-term illness. Whether it's a toddler with a fever or a teen with the flu, we pray it will pass quickly and the child will rise healthy. I've included this section to cover our children with scriptural prayer when they need healing. Remember, one of the names of God is Jehovah Rapha, "the God Who Heals." It's who He is. It's what He does.

• • •

> He was pierced for our transgressions, he was crushed for
> our iniquities; the punishment that brought us peace was
> on him, and by his wounds we are healed. (Isaiah 53:5)

Father, Your Word tells us that Jesus was pierced for our rebellion and crushed for our sin, that He was beaten so that we could have peace and flogged so that we could be healed. I don't understand how all that works, but I believe when You say that by His stripes we are healed. I pray by Jesus' stripes my child will be healed.

> Praise the LORD, my soul, and forget not all his benefits—who forgives all your sins and heals all your diseases, who redeems your life from the pit and crowns you with love and compassion, who satisfies your desires with good things so that your youth is renewed like the eagle's. (Psalm 103:2–5)

Thank You for the many benefits we have as believers, two of which are the forgiveness of sins and healing from diseases. I pray You will heal my child and renew their strength like the strength of eagles.

> Jesus went through all the towns and villages, teaching in their synagogues, proclaiming the good news of the kingdom and healing every disease and sickness. (Matthew 9:35)

Father, just as Jesus went through all the towns and villages, healing every disease and sickness, I pray You will heal my child in Jesus' name. Just as You made the blind to see, the lame to walk, the deaf to hear, the leprous skin to be made whole, the bleeding to cease, the bent and bowed to stand tall, the withered hand to unfurl, and the dead to rise, I pray You will heal my child's body and make them whole.

Jesus Christ is the same yesterday and today and forever. (Hebrews 13:8)

Your Word tells me that You are the same yesterday, today, and forever. I praise Your name and stand on the promises that the miracles You performed in times past You still perform today.

When Jesus landed and saw a large crowd, he had compassion on them and healed their sick. (Matthew 14:14)

Lord, just as you had compassion on the sick when You walked this earth, I pray You will have compassion on my child and heal them quickly.

Jesus said to her, "Woman, you have great faith! Your request is granted." And her daughter was healed at that moment. (Matthew 15:28)

Just as the Canaanite mother asked and kept on asking for You to heal her daughter, I ask and keep on asking, fully believing that You are able to heal my child.

When Jesus entered the synagogue leader's house and saw the noisy crowd and people playing pipes, he said, "Go away. The girl is not dead but asleep." But they laughed at him. After the crowd had been put outside, he went in and took the girl by the hand, and she got up. (Matthew 9:23–25)

Father, just as Jairus asked Jesus to heal his twelve-year-old daughter, I ask You to heal my child. Even if others laugh at my faith or make fun of my belief, I will shut out the doubters and trust in You. I pray You will take my child by the hand and that they will get up and be well.

> One of the names of God is Jehovah Rapha, "the God Who Heals." It's who He is. It's what He does.

The centurion replied, "Lord, I do not deserve to have you come under my roof. But just say the word, and my servant will be healed...." Then Jesus said to the centurion, "Go! Let it be done just as you believed it would." And his servant was healed at that moment. (Matthew 8:8, 13)

Lord, I pray You will just say the word ... just say the word. I intercede on my child's behalf, asking You to command sickness, infirmity, and disease to leave their body. Please restore their health and renew their strength. I pray it will be done and believe it will be.

[Jesus said,] I will do whatever you ask in my name, so that the Father may be glorified in the Son. You may ask me for anything in my name, and I will do it. (John 14:13–14)

Lord, Your Word says I may ask You for anything in Your name and You will do it. I know this means that I can ask for anything that is according to Your will and in alignment with Your purposes. With that in mind, I pray You will heal my child. And if it is not Your perfect will for my child to be healed at this time, give us both the assurance that Your grace is sufficient, for Your power is made perfect in our weakness.

Nothing will be impossible with God. (Luke 1:37 ESV)

Finally, Lord, I know that nothing is impossible with You. No matter what my friends, family, or doctors may tell me, I know You can heal my child quickly, totally, and completely. I believe in miracles. I believe in You. In Jesus' name, amen.

Prayer for Salvation

As I have mentioned earlier in this prayer journey, the most important decision our children will ever make is to accept Jesus Christ as Lord and Savior—all else pales in comparison. I have included a few prayers for salvation in the thirty days of prayer, but for those who would like to focus on this one crucial decision with eternal consequences, I've included this section targeting your child's salvation.

Prayer has mighty power to prepare the heart for the precious seed of truth to be planted. Prayer has supernatural strength to demolish strongholds of the enemy that hold the sinner captive. Prayer has the potential to speak to the mountain of unbelief and cast it into the sea.

Remember, when you pray the Word of God, you pray the will of God. And God does not want "anyone to perish, but everyone to come to repentance" (2 Peter 3:9).

● ● ●

He [Jesus] told them, "The harvest is plentiful, but the workers are few. Ask the Lord of the harvest, therefore, to send out workers into his harvest field." (Luke 10:2)

Heavenly Father, I ask You to send people into my child's life to till the soil of their heart, to plant the seeds of truth, to water with prayer, and to bring in the harvest. Just as You sent Paul to the young Timothy, I pray You will place people in my child's path who will guide them to see, hear, and know Jesus as Savior and Lord.

> God demonstrates his own love for us in this: While we were still sinners, Christ died for us. (Romans 5:8)

Gracious God, please open my child's eyes and heart to the truth that You have demonstrated Your love for them by sending Your Son to die for them. Let my child know that they don't have to get life tidied up before they come to You. Remind them that You accept them just as they are—mess and all.

> God so loved the world that he gave his one and only Son, that whoever believes in him shall not perish but have eternal life. (John 3:16)

> The Son of Man came to seek and to save the lost. (Luke 19:10)

Lord, thank You for loving my child so much that You gave Your one and only Son as a sacrifice for their sins. Thank You for Jesus' willingness to take on the form of human flesh and die on Calvary's cross. Thank You that Jesus came to seek and to save my child. I pray they will turn away from sin and toward You. Move their heart to believe on the Lord Jesus and be saved.

> [Jesus said,] The thief comes only to steal and kill and destroy; I came so that they would have life, and have it abundantly. (John 10:10 NASB)

> The reason the Son of God appeared was to destroy the devil's work. (1 John 3:8b)

Father, I know that the enemy would like nothing better than to steal, kill, and destroy the plans and purposes You have for my child. Thank You for sending Your Son to destroy the devil's work that began in the garden of Eden. I pray against the power of the enemy in Jesus' name. Release the Holy Spirit to thwart the enemy's tactics, destroy the enemy's strongholds, and render the enemy impotent. I pray, almighty God, that You will destroy the devil's work in my child's life—that You will tear down the walls, cut loose the shackles, and illuminate the darkness. I pray my child will come to saving faith in Jesus and experience abundant life on earth and eternal life in heaven.

> [Jesus said,] Very truly I tell you, whoever hears my word and believes him who sent me has eternal life and will not be judged but has crossed over from death to life. (John 5:24)

I pray my child will hear the Word of truth and believe in Christ the Lord. Even though they may not understand all of what it means to be a Christian, I pray they will simply say yes to what they do know. I pray they will believe by faith.

If you confess with your mouth that Jesus is Lord and believe in your heart that God raised him from the dead, you will be saved. For with the heart one believes and is justified, and with the mouth one confesses and is saved.... For "everyone who calls on the name of the Lord will be saved." (Romans 10:9–10, 13 ESV)

I pray my child will confess with their mouth, "Jesus is Lord," and believe in their heart that You raised Him from the dead. I pray in faith that they will call on the name of the Lord Jesus and be saved. Lord, Your Word says we can ask anything according to Your will and You will do it. I stand on that promise for my child.

> Prayer has mighty power to prepare the heart for the precious seed of truth to be planted.

If the Good News we preach is hidden behind a veil, it is hidden only from people who are perishing. Satan, who is the god of this world, has blinded the minds of those who

don't believe. They are unable to see the glorious light
of the Good News. They don't understand this message
about the glory of Christ, who is the exact likeness of
God. (2 Corinthians 4:3–4 NLT)

Lord, if there is anything keeping my child from understanding and
believing the truth of the gospel, I ask You to remove it. Open my child's
eyes to see the glorious light of the good news—the light of the gospel
that shines through Christ. Open my child's mind to Your truth and my
child's heart to Your love.

The Lord is not slow in keeping his promise, as some
understand slowness. Instead he is patient with you, not
wanting anyone to perish, but everyone to come to repentance. (2 Peter 3:9)

Father, help me not to grow anxious when it feels like time is rushing by
without my child deciding to follow You. I know that You are not slow in
keeping Your promise but are always right on time. Thank You for being
patient with my child. Help me to do the same.

God our Savior … wants all people to be saved and to
come to a knowledge of the truth. (1 Timothy 2:3b–4)

God, Your Word says that You want everyone to come to repentance—
that means everyone. Your Word says You want all people to be saved and
to come to a knowledge of the truth—that means all people. Therefore,
I know You want my child to come to repentance, to be saved, and to

come to a knowledge of the truth. I pray You will do whatever is necessary to bring them to saving faith. I'm holding on and trusting You, fully persuaded that You will finish what You have started in them.

> [Jesus said,] Here I am! I stand at the door and knock. If anyone hears my voice and opens the door, I will come in and eat with that person, and they with me. (Revelation 3:20)

Jesus, I pray my child will sense You knocking on the door of their heart. Make them sensitive to Your persistent tapping, and throw the door wide open. I pray You will make Yourself at home in my child's heart.

Prayer for the Prodigal

Myles grew up in a Christian home with praying parents. He dutifully went to church, learned about Jesus, and had all the right answers to the religious questions. His parents, Mike and Ross Ann, described Myles as a fun, happy, hardworking boy who filled their lives with joy. But during his junior year in high school, all that changed. Myles drifted away from the faith. He went through the motions at church, but his heart was far away from God. As a result, he began to choose different friends, dark activities, and diverse vices to fill a void he couldn't even explain.

His mom cried out, "God, what did we do wrong!" But it wasn't anything that Ross Ann or Mike had done wrong at all. This was part of Myles's journey ... part of his story. What they did do was everything right ... they continued praying that God would bring Myles to his knees. Claiming Scripture. Interceding faithfully. Believing powerfully.

Five years later, in a hotel room thousands of miles from home, Myles fell on his bed after a night of partying. Life wasn't working. Shots of vodka couldn't dull the pain. The next high left him lower than before. Lying across his bed, Myles looked over at his bedside table and saw a Bible.

He picked it up and cried out to God, "Lord, please show me what it means to follow You. I want to know You. I'm empty. There is nothing in this world that will fill this void. I'm broken."

"And that's where God met me," Myles now explains. "I'm so thankful for praying parents."

Knees. That is the landmark that brings you to praying for your child's relationship with God. Bending their knees in humility breaks the chains of pride and sets them free to experience the abundant life on earth and eternal life in heaven that Jesus came to give.

James reminds us, "Humble yourselves in the sight of the Lord, and He will lift you up" (James 4:10 NKJV). The Amplified Bible, Classic Edition, puts it this way, "Humble yourselves [feeling very insignificant] in the presence of the Lord, and He will exalt you [He will lift you up and make your lives significant]" (AMPC).

> God knows all about prodigals ... and He loves them.

The opposite of humility is pride. Webster defines *pride* as "exaggerated self-esteem."[1] It is a type of self-worship that takes full credit for one's accomplishments, resources, and successes. Pride was what caused Satan to fall from heaven (Ezekiel 28), Saul to lose his reign over Israel (1 Samuel 13), and King Uzziah to be cursed with leprosy (2 Chronicles 26:16–22). Pride makes a person refuse to bend the knee in submission to God, stunts spiritual growth, and stymies passion for Christ.

When we think of a prodigal, usually a young adult comes to mind. However, with children exposed to more forces outside the home than ever before, that prodigal may be a teen or a preteen. I've included this section for the parent whose child made a commitment to Jesus at an early age but then rebelled against or became complacent about all things spiritual. This is for the parent whose child enjoyed being a part of a Christian community or church activities but fell in with a rebellious crowd and turned their back on Christ. For the parent whose child was on the right road spiritually but then took a sharp turn in the opposite direction.

Studies show that 66 percent of young adults between the ages of eighteen to twenty-two stop attending church regularly (twice a month or more) for at least a year.[2] We all know young adults who were raised in Christian homes with Christian values who have walked away from the faith.

Let me give you a holy hug right now. Our job as parents is to "train up a child in the way [they] should go" (Proverbs 22:6 ESV); however, the decisions they make are their own. God is the perfect parent and look how His children rebelled all through Scripture. Don't allow the enemy to place the burden of your prodigal's rebellion on your shoulders. It is not yours to carry but to cast. "Cast your burden on the LORD" (Psalm 55:22 ESV).

God knows all about prodigals … and He loves them. So don't lose heart. Let's pray them home.

● ● ●

I am certain that God, who began the good work within
you, will continue his work until it is finally finished on the
day when Christ Jesus returns. (Philippians 1:6 NLT)

God, I am confident of this: You began a good work in my child, and
You will complete it. You will finish what You started. My prayer is
that my child will move from rebellion against You to repentance
before You to reestablishing their relationship with You … sooner
rather than later.

Immediately, something like scales fell from Saul's eyes, and
he could see again. He got up and was baptized, and after
taking some food, he regained his strength. (Acts 9:18–19a)

Lord, there seems to be scales over my child's eyes, preventing them from
seeing the truth. I pray You will remove those scales and remove the
spiritual blindness that has taken hold of them. Open my prodigal's eyes
to see, repent, and return.

When he finally came to his senses, he said to himself, "At
home even the hired servants have food enough to spare,
and here I am dying of hunger!" (Luke 15:17 NLT)

I pray my child, like the Prodigal Son in Jesus' parable, will realize that
they are powerless to make it in this life apart from Christ. Give them
a gnawing hunger that the world can't satisfy. I pray they will come to
their senses and come back to You.

Jesus looked at them and said, "With man this is impossible, but with God all things are possible." (Matthew 19:26)

Father, I know there is nothing I can say or do that will bring my prodigal back except pray. There's no amount of debating, cajoling, or convincing that will open their closed heart. Only You can do that. So I pray and give this burden to You, knowing that what is impossible for man is possible with You.

Where can I go from your Spirit? Where can I flee from your presence? If I go up to the heavens, you are there; if I make my bed in the depths, you are there. If I rise on the wings of the dawn, if I settle on the far side of the sea, even there your hand will guide me, your right hand will hold me fast. (Psalm 139:7–10)

Hallelujah! There is nowhere my child can go to escape Your presence. You are in every car, at every party, in every dark room. I pray the Holy Spirit will stalk my child—that He will go right along with them into every situation and relationship so they will feel uncomfortable and convicted.

I will give them an undivided heart and put a new spirit in them; I will remove from them their heart of stone and give them a heart of flesh. Then they will follow my decrees and be careful to keep my laws. They will be my people, and I will be their God. (Ezekiel 11:19–20)

I pray You will give my child an undivided heart and put a new spirit in them. Even though they decided to follow You at one time, they now have a divided heart that vacillates between following You and following the world. Lord, change my child's heart. Remove the rebellious heart of stone, and give them a repentant heart of flesh. I pray they will once again follow You and Your ways.

> Start children off on the way they should go, and even when they are old they will not turn from it. (Proverbs 22:6)

Lord, I know that a proverb is not a promise but a wise saying. And I know my child has free will. However, I pray the wisdom of this proverb will hold true for my child. I'm thankful they have been trained up in the ways they should go. I pray my child will return to that way and live fully and free in Christ.

> He reached down from on high and took hold of me; he drew me out of deep waters. He rescued me from my powerful enemy, from my foes, who were too strong for me. They confronted me in the day of my disaster, but the LORD was my support. He brought me out into a spacious place; he rescued me because he delighted in me. (Psalm 18:16–19)

I pray You will reach down from on high and take hold of my child; draw them out of the deep waters of rebellion and set them on the dry land of repentance. I ask You to rescue my child from the powerful enemies—the devil and evils forces who seek to pull them away from Christianity. Be their support even when they don't know they need it. I pray You will bring my child out from the confines of bondage and into the spacious land of freedom. Thank You for loving my child even more than I do.

> Though we live in the world, we do not wage war as the world does. The weapons we fight with are not the weapons of the world. On the contrary, they have divine power to demolish strongholds. (2 Corinthians 10:3–4)

Father, thank You for the power of the Holy Spirit that lives in every believer. I pray now, in the power of the Holy Spirit and the name of Jesus, that You will demolish any strongholds in my child's life that are pulling them away from You and toward the world. I pray against the spirits of rebellion, pride, sensuality, addiction, and anger. I pray against every proud obstacle that keeps my child from following you.

> [Jesus said,] I have pleaded in prayer for you, Simon, that your faith should not fail. So when you have repented and turned to me again, strengthen your brothers. (Luke 22:32 NLT)

Oh Father, just as Peter walked away from Jesus during His time of need, my child has walked away from Him as well. I am so encouraged that Jesus not only forgave Peter but also pursued him, confronted him, and welcomed him back. I pray the same words for my child that Jesus spoke to Peter by the fire: "When you have repented and turned to [Jesus] again, strengthen your brothers." I pray my child will one day use how they turned back to God to help others who are in a period of rebellion turn back to You as well.

When Feeling Discouraged or Depressed

My son, Steven, was in the seventh grade, taking advanced math, advanced English, advanced science, and Latin. It was also his first year playing on a school sports team, and he got home about six o'clock every night. Nothing was going well. It was hard to get his schoolwork done when he came home exhausted. A few times he had worked hard on an assignment only to find that he had done the wrong page. Latin was Greek to him, and there was no sign he was going to catch on anytime soon.

One day after practice, I heard him in the shower, crying out to God, "Lord, I'm not good at anything. Just help me be good at something. Just one thing."

As you can imagine, that broke my heart. Actually, Steven was good at many things, but in his mind, the negative far outweighed the positive. After praying for guidance, I met with the principal and took Steven out of advanced Latin with cheers all around. But his discouragement really turned around when I received a written note from one of his teachers who knew he was struggling with disappointment and discouragement.

Dear Mr. and Mrs. Jaynes,

Steven has been doing excellent work in science. His name has been at the top of the list on recent tests and quizzes. No doubt he told you about his perfect score on our last test. He is a fine young man. I would love a room full of Stevens!

Best Regards,

Mrs. Connie Roads

Though this note of encouragement was addressed to Steven's dad and me, it was really for our son—this teacher knew we would read it to him. She looked past the tough exterior of adolescence and saw a disappointed and discouraged soul. I have no doubt that her prayers and mine intersected in heaven and God prompted her to take up pen and paper. Steven's discouragement lifted, his fun personality returned, and he finished seventh grade well.

It is so difficult to watch a child fall into a season or discouragement or depression. The dictionary defines *discouragement* as "dispiritedness or lack of confidence, enthusiasm."[3] Most likely you know for yourself what that feels and looks like.

Clinical depression is a mood disorder that causes a persistent feeling of sadness and loss of interest that can interfere with your daily activities. If you sense your child is clinically depressed, I encourage you to pray and seek medical intervention. However, one can have periods of depression that aren't a clinical disorder but simply sadness with the temporary loss of joy. God has a special place in His heart for the child with the broken heart. So let's pray for our children whom God longs to raise out of the pit of discouragement and set on solid ground.

He lifted me out of the pit of despair, out of the mud and
the mire. He set my feet on solid ground and steadied me
as I walked along. (Psalm 40:2 NLT)

Father, I ask You to lift my child out of the pit of sadness and set their
feet on the solid ground of joy. Reach in and pull them out. Give them
the hope that life will be better than what they are experiencing at the
present time.

He has given me a new song to sing, a hymn of praise to
our God. Many will see what he has done and be amazed.
They will put their trust in the LORD. (Psalm 40:3 NLT)

God, I sense my child has lost their joy. I pray You will put a new song
of joy in their heart. I pray they will hear the tune of praise and begin to
hum along. I know the idea of a joyful, grateful heart is a far cry from
where my child is right now, but I also know that You are a miracle-
working God, who, as Romans 4:17 says, "calls into existence the things
that do not exist" [ESV].

You, LORD, are a shield around me, my glory, the One
who lifts my head high. (Psalm 3:3)

Lord, right now, my child's countenance has fallen low with disappointment, dejection, and defeat. I pray You will place Your holy hand under
their chin and lift their head out of the gloom. Open my child's eyes to
see a way forward and their heart to find the joy of living.

The righteous cry out, and the LORD hears them; he delivers them from all their troubles. The LORD is close to the brokenhearted and saves those who are crushed in spirit. (Psalm 34:17–18)

Father, Your Word tells us that when the righteous cry for help, You hear and deliver them out of all their troubles. I am crying out on my child's behalf. My child is deeply discouraged, so I stand on the promise that You are near the brokenhearted and save the crushed in spirit. Lift their broken spirit. Breathe new life into their saddened soul. Deliver them from a spirit of depression, and give them a spirit of joy.

He heals the brokenhearted and binds up their wounds. (Psalm 147:3)

Thank You, God, for healing the brokenhearted and binding up their wounds. I pray You will heal my child's disappointed heart and bandage their wounded soul.

Even youths will become weak and tired, and young men will fall in exhaustion. But those who trust in the LORD will find new strength. They will soar high on wings like eagles. They will run and not grow weary. They will walk and not faint. (Isaiah 40:30–31 NLT)

God, right now my child has become weak, weary, tired, and tapped out. I pray they will turn to You, trust in You, and find new strength in

You. Refresh and reenergize my child's spirit so that they will soar like the eagles—not flapping their wings, trying to make life work on their own, but relying on the rising current of Your strength to lift them and make them fly.

> Brothers and sisters, whatever is true, whatever is noble, whatever is right, whatever is pure, whatever is lovely, whatever is admirable—if anything is excellent or praise-worthy—think about such things. (Philippians 4:8)

Lord, my child has so many negative thoughts running through their mind right now. I know that what we think about, we become. Therefore, I pray they will cease having distorted, negative opinions about their identity and reality. Help them have a clear, positive outlook about who they are and what the future holds. Replace their gloomy attitude with a glad countenance, their pessimistic outlook with optimistic anticipation, and a sense of hopelessness with a renewed sense of happiness.

> "I know the plans I have for you," declares the LORD, "plans to prosper you and not to harm you, plans to give you hope and a future." (Jeremiah 29:11)

I pray my child will not compare their failures to someone else's successes. Help them focus on all they do have rather than on what they don't have. Help them see the unique ways that You have formed and fashioned them for success.

> I will lead the blind by ways they have not known, along
> unfamiliar paths I will guide them; I will turn the dark-
> ness into light before them and make the rough places
> smooth. These are the things I will do; I will not forsake
> them. (Isaiah 42:16)

Father, right now my child is blind to all the ways You have blessed them. I pray You will take them by the hand and guide them out of this darkness and into the light. I ask that You make the rough places smooth, the difficult relationships congenial, and the challenging circumstances manageable.

> You have turned my mourning into joyful dancing. You
> have taken away my clothes of mourning and clothed
> me with joy, that I might sing praises to you and not be
> silent. O LORD my God, I will give you thanks forever!
> (Psalm 30:11–12 NLT)

Finally, Lord, I claim and proclaim that You will turn my child's mourning into joyful dancing and take away their clothes of mourning and replace them with clothes of joy. I pray that my child will come out of this dark place singing praises to You and giving thanks forever! In Jesus' name, amen.

Acknowledgments

I've often said that writing a book is like putting together a giant jigsaw puzzle without the box top as a guide. Some people provide the corners and some the sides, while a host of others give hints about the marriage of shapes that fill the places in between. A special thanks to the following people for making *Praying for Your Child* a reality:

The Esther Press team: Susan McPherson for her enthusiastic vision of Esther Press and gracious invite to be part of the team. Stephanie Bennett for herding cats and keeping us focused, organized, and on time. Judy Gillispie for dotting all the i's and crossing all the t's to make this book the best it could be. James Hershberger for his artistic genius in cover design. Susan Murdock for her special touches in the lovely interior design. Rudy Kish, Annette Brickbealer, and Angie Carlen—the marketing marvels.

God's Girls Mastermind Group, who prayed me through: Carol Kent, Rachel Wojo, Julie Gillies, Pat Layton, Pam Farrel, and Jill Savage. I have learned so much from each of you.

Bill Jensen, my friend and agent extraordinaire, for his wisdom and guidance.

Mike McKee, Ross Ann McKee, Myles McKee, Anna Groome, Grace Anne Vick, and Katie Signaigo for allowing me to share your stories with moms around the world.

Steven, my son, who taught me everything I know about being a mom.

Steve, my husband, for being my chief cheerleader in life and in love.

God the Father, who equips me; God the Son, who envelops me; and God the Hoy Spirit, who empowers me. I pray the words of my mouth, the meditations of my heart, and the ink in my pen will honor You and help mothers all around the world know how to pray purposefully and powerfully for their children.

Notes

Chapter 1: The Battle for Our Children

1. Charles Spurgeon, *Twelve Sermons on Prayer* (Grand Rapids, MI: Baker Book House, 1971), 31.

2. *New Lexicon Webster's Dictionary of the English Language* (New York: Lexicon, 1989), s.v. "lavish."

3. Jennifer Kennedy Dean, *The Praying Life* (Birmingham, AL: Woman's Missionary Union, 1997), 34.

4. Sharon Jaynes, *When You Don't Like Your Story: What If Your Worst Chapters Could Become Your Greatest Victories?* (Nashville, TN: Thomas Nelson, 2021), 30–31.

5. S. D. Gordon, *Quiet Talks on Prayer* (1904; repr. New York: Cosimo, 2005), 16.

6. Larry S. Clark, "The Warrior," unpublished poem, 1993; taken directly from a signed copy that the poet presented to the author.

Chapter 2: The Landmarks of Prayer

1. "Brain Development," First Things First, accessed February 16, 2023, www.firstthingsfirst.org/early-childhood-matters/brain-development.

2. Jonathan Rothwell, "You Are What You Watch: The Social Effects of TV," *New York Times*, July 25, 2019, www.nytimes.com/2019/07/25/upshot/social -effects-television.html.

3. Roy H. Williams, "An Energy of Words," Roy H. Williams Marketing, April 19, 2000, www.rhw.com/2000/04/19/an-energy-of-words.

4. "What Do Children Worry About?: A Fact Sheet for Teachers and Parents," Cornell Cooperative Extension, accessed February 16, 2023, http://cceoneida.com/resources/what-kids-worry-about.

5. *New Lexicon Webster's Dictionary of the English Language* (New York: Lexicon, 1989), s.v. "strength."

6. Linda Klepacki, "What Your Teens Need to Know about Sex," Focus on the Family, February 1, 2005, www.focusonthefamily.com/lifechallenges/love-and-sex /purity/what-your-teens-need-to-know-about-sex.

Chapter 3: How to Use This Book

1. W. E. Vine, Merrrill F. Unger, and William White Jr., *Vine's Complete Expository Dictionary of Old and New Testament Words* (Nashville, TN: Thomas Nelson, 1985), 20.

Appendix: Prayer for the Prodigal

1. *Merriam-Webster.com Dictionary*, s.v. "pride," accessed February 20, 2023, www.merriam-webster.com/dictionary/pride.

2. Aaron Earls, "Most Teenagers Drop Out of Church When They Become Young Adults," Lifeway Research, January 15, 2019, https://research.lifeway.com/2019/01 /15/most-teenagers-drop-out-of-church-as-young-adults.

3. *Oxford Thesaurus of English*, 3rd ed. (2009), s.v. "discouragement."